LIFE NATURE LIBRARY

THE LAND AND WILDLIFE OF

NORTH AMERICA

TIME-LIFE BOOKS

LIFE WORLD LIBRARY

LIFE NATURE LIBRARY

LIFE SCIENCE LIBRARY

THE LIFE HISTORY OF THE UNITED STATES

LIFE PICTORIAL ATLAS OF THE WORLD

THE EPIC OF MAN

THE WONDERS OF LIFE ON EARTH

THE WORLD WE LIVE IN

THE WORLD'S GREAT RELIGIONS

THE LIFE BOOK OF CHRISTMAS

LIFE'S PICTURE HISTORY OF WESTERN MAN

THE LIFE TREASURY OF AMERICAN FOLKLORE

AMERICA'S ARTS AND SKILLS

THE SECOND WORLD WAR

LIFE'S PICTURE HISTORY OF WORLD WAR II

PICTURE COOK BOOK

LIFE GUIDE TO PARIS

LIFE NATURE LIBRARY

THE LAND AND WILDLIFE OF
NORTH AMERICA

by Peter Farb
and The Editors of LIFE

TIME INCORPORATED
NEW YORK

A
STONEHENGE
BOOK

About the Author

Peter Farb's panoramic knowledge of nature has prompted the editors of the LIFE Nature Library to call upon him to write an unprecedented fourth volume for the series. Eminently qualified as he was to author *The Forest*, *The Insects* and *Ecology*, he is equally well equipped to discuss North America—his *Face of North America: The Natural History of a Continent* was a 1963 Book-of-the-Month Club selection and one of the books presented by the late President John F. Kennedy to the heads of 100 foreign governments. Mr. Farb also serves as the Curator of American Indian Cultures for the Riverside Museum in New York City, where in 1964 he assembled an exhibit on Pueblo Indian paintings that is now touring major American museums. He is now working on a comprehensive book on American Indians and is also editor and coauthor of Harper & Row's forthcoming North American Nature series.

ON THE COVER: Feeding placidly in a northern lake, moose, with their huge antlers, are the very symbol of America's deep woods. The moose is a browser, equipped to feed on high willow branches as well as on the lush underwater growth. These majestic creatures are the largest antlered animals that ever have lived on earth.

Contents

TIME-LIFE BOOKS

EDITOR
Norman P. Ross
TEXT DIRECTOR   ART DIRECTOR
William Jay Gold   Edward A. Hamilton
CHIEF OF RESEARCH
Beatrice T. Dobie
Assistant Text Director: Jerry Korn
Assistant Chief of Research: Monica O. Horne

•

PUBLISHER
Rhett Austell
General Manager: John A. Watters
Business Manager: John D. McSweeney
Circulation Manager: Joan D. Lanning

LIFE MAGAZINE

EDITOR: Edward K. Thompson
MANAGING EDITOR: George P. Hunt
PUBLISHER: Jerome S. Hardy

LIFE NATURE LIBRARY

EDITOR: Maitland A. Edey
Associate Editor: Percy Knauth
Assistants to the Editor: Robert Morton, John Porter
Designer: Paul Jensen
Staff Writers: Dale Brown, Timothy Carr, Mary Louise Grossman, Peter Wood
Chief Researcher: Martha Turner
Researchers: Jane Alexander, David Bridge, Doris Bry, Peggy Bushong, Yvonne Chan, Joan Chasin, Eleanor Feltser, Nancy Jacobsen, Nancy Newman, Paula Norworth, Carol Phillippe, Marjorie Pickens, Susan Rayfield, Carollee Rosenblatt, Roxanna Sayre, Nancy Shuker, Iris Unger, John von Hartz

EDITORIAL PRODUCTION
Art Associate: Robert L. Young
Art Assistants: James D. Smith, Mark A. Binn, John Newcomb
Picture Researchers: Margaret K. Goldsmith, Susan Boyle
Copy Staff: Marian Gordon Goldman, Joan Chambers, Dolores A. Littles

The text for this book was written by Peter Farb, the picture essays by the editorial staff. The following individuals and departments of Time Incorporated were helpful in producing the book: Eliot Elisofon, Albert Fenn, Fritz Goro, Dmitri Kessel and George Silk, LIFE staff photographers; Doris O'Neil, Chief, LIFE Picture Library; Richard M. Clurman, Chief, TIME-LIFE News Service; and Content Peckham, Chief, Time Incorporated Bureau of Editorial Reference.

Introduction

"There are some who can live without wild things, and some who cannot . . . Like winds and sunsets, wild things were taken for granted until progress began to do away with them. Now we face the question whether a still higher 'standard of living' is worth its cost in things natural, wild, and free. For us of the minority, the opportunity to see geese is more important than television, and the chance to find a pasque-flower is a right as inalienable as free speech."—ALDO LEOPOLD, *A Sand County Almanac, 1949.*

EACH generation has a scientific elite that discovers new truths about the natural world. On our continent, the exciting work of discovering, collecting and classifying the flora and fauna was performed by the Bartrams and Audubons of yesteryear. The Bartrams of today—men like Aldo Leopold, Olaus Murie and Paul Sears, and women like Rachel Carson—have been discoverers of a different order, trained in geology, biology or geography; but invariably they have derived deep insight from their grasp of the sensitive science of ecology, which teaches us, in John Muir's words, that "when we try to pick out anything by itself, we find it hitched to everything else in the universe."

Peter Farb, a young man with a consuming interest in land and living things, is already one of the finest conservation spokesmen of our period. He understands the interrelationships of all resources, and he is obviously fascinated by the catalytic role, for good or for ill, of man himself. He has tied this wildlife story to the history of American exploration   and we get a clear picture of the intoxicating influence of resource abundance that trapped the American pioneers from the very beginning in a myth of superabundance. He records the feats of the settlers who cut, shot and burned their way across the virgin spaces, and he spells out the effects on things wild and free. He gently mocks us as he recalls that wolverines were long ago extirpated from Michigan, the "Wolverine State"; and he describes in detail the pressures and policies that have produced landscapes where today only the hardy few can get a glimpse of an elk, a grizzly, a bighorn, a moose or a wolf. Nor does he spare us the peril in which we have put such marvelous birds as the whooping crane and the California condor.

But there are hopeful notes. Peter Farb suggests that science now enables us to repair the damage of the past and literally to "re-create" the virginal conditions of the past in parts of our landscape. One hopes he is indeed prescient, for the passage of the Wilderness Bill this year could arouse new respect for wilderness and wildlife values and produce a new flowering of our conservation conscience. Who can say, once we set out to re-create primeval nature, what future generations might achieve in refreshing and restoring the face of North America?

Peter Farb is one of that growing number who cannot live without wild things. It is my hope that books like this one will rejuvenate the conservation cause and help us save and restore the grandeur of the American continent.

STEWART L. UDALL
Secretary of the Interior

THE PEACE RIVER IN BRITISH COLUMBIA, HERE UNMARRED BY DAMS AND MODERN INDUSTRY, TYPIFIES THE WIDE VALLEY ROUTES FOLLOWED FROM

1   A Virgin Continent

THE BERING LAND BRIDGE BY EARLY MEN FROM ASIA. SPREADING IN ALL DIRECTIONS, THEY FINALLY PEOPLED BOTH NORTH AND SOUTH AMERICA

I THINKE in all the world the like abundance is not to be found.'' These words were written by an English sea captain named Arthur Barlowe shortly after his discovery of Virginia in 1584. Now, nearly 400 years later, they have the ring of a prophecy fulfilled, for they were among the first ever to be set down about the New World by somebody sent here to judge its prospects for settlement and trade—instead of merely as a source of gold, as was the practice of the Spaniards who preceded Barlowe.

Barlowe's job was to look at the land itself, the things that grew on it and the animals it supported. He was an agent for one of the most remarkable men of his age, the enterpriser and global dreamer Sir Walter Raleigh, who was ahead of most of his contemporaries in realizing that the true wealth of the new continent probably lay in its timber, its wildlife and its fertile soil rather than in its mineral resources. Barlowe did not disappoint his patron. His report overflows with a sense of wonder at the incredible plenitude of life that he found. He reported shores "so full of grapes, as the very beating and surge of the Sea owerflowed them . . . Deere, Conies, Hares and fowle . . . in incredible abundance. . . . The soil is the most plentifull, sweete, fruitfull and wholsome of all the worlde." As a seafarer from a country where trees suitable for shipbuilding had been heavily logged, he did not overlook "about fourteen seuerall sweete smelling timber trees. . . . the highest and reddest Cedars of the world," and oaks "farre greater and better" than grew in England.

Captain Barlowe's reaction to his first sight of North America was typical of that of many other early explorers. Wherever these men touched the Atlantic, Gulf and Pacific shores or even ventured a short distance inland, the new continent seemed to promise an unbelievable abundance of life. Yet they stood merely on the outskirts of a newly found wilderness and could not visualize the extent and diversity of this land mass. Spaniards on the southern shore found morasses and swamps, Englishmen probing the Atlantic coast encountered the fringes of a great deciduous forest, Frenchmen coming down the St. Lawrence River caught a glimpse of the coniferous forest. None of them could know that, farther inland, there towered trees whose trunks surpassed the height of the highest shipmasts, and green forests that harbored mammals whose fur was as soft and beautiful as any in the world. Far beyond their ken, in the grassy heart of the continent were unsuspected herds of bison and pronghorn, their numbers uncountable and seemingly inexhaustible. The streams and lakes swarmed with multitudes of fishes and mollusks, and at times the skies were blackened by dense clouds of birds. The explorers had truly found a "plenty" which Barlowe had not imagined existed anywhere else on the planet.

THIS book is concerned with the Nearctic realm, which is that part of the North American continent from the high plateau of southern Mexico northward. And we know that the continent was indeed richly endowed—with tens of thousands of plant species, upward of 800 kinds of birds, more than 400 mammals, and at least 340 kinds of reptiles and amphibians. And it all lay before the Europeans merely for the taking.

In telling the story of the North American continent, one is tempted to conjure up a picture of it in its pristine state or perhaps to linger over the few wilderness remnants that survive for today's American. But in this book the story of North America is approached from a different viewpoint. In sadness and in shame, here is chronicled the primeval bounty of the continent at the time of its discovery—and how its rich fabric of life became a thing of shreds and patches within only a few centuries. Relying on the narratives of early explorers, trappers and settlers, it is possible in the imagination to recapture the bounty of the virgin continent—but also to hear the ringing of axes, the crackle of fire, the whine of bullets, the snap of steel traps that have sent echoes of the decimation of that bounty reverberating into the present century.

In the past 200 years, North America has lost more bird species than any other continental area; only remnants of the great primeval deciduous forests survive in isolated patches; the rich expanse of the prairies now is almost deserted by wild animals; the once-clear rivers are now so polluted that scarcely a pure river remains in the United States.

Those explorers who saw the continent in its primeval splendor often were awed by the plenty of the land but, surprisingly, they showed little wonder at the kinds of mammals, birds, trees and humans that populated it. In truth, the life of North America looked somewhat, but not exactly, like the animals and plants familiar in Europe. Rather than stepping into a totally strange world, as Europeans did when they discovered Australia and South America, the explorers of North America found a partly familiar one. Many of the mammals, birds and reptiles appeared eerily similar to those known in Eurasia, yet intangibly different. There are good reasons for both the similarity and the differences.

ALTHOUGH the subject of the development of North America's wildlife is an extremely involved one, it is based on a couple of simple facts. One of the most important of these is that many of the animals found on the continent today are quite recent arrivals from other places. This does not mean that *nothing* lived here in the distant past. On the contrary, North America, like every other continent, had its early history of lower forms of life, followed by the development of amphibians, huge reptiles, birds and many kinds of primitive and protomammals, all now extinct. But this long and complex story does not concern us in this book. What we are discussing is the period of the Tertiary, starting about 60 million years ago and lasting until one million years ago. At that time many of the ancestors of our present animals began walking in—from Asia. Today North America seems isolated from the great Eurasian land mass, with 56 miles of choppy water separating Siberia and Alaska at their closest points, but this was not always the case. During part of the Tertiary, Alaska and Siberia were joined by a land bridge which at times was more than a thousand miles wide, and animals entered North America simply by walking across it. There was heavy traffic in both directions, invasion and spread, evolution and extinction. Over the bridge traveled the ancestors of modern horses, camels, tapirs, opossums, wild dogs, cats, weasels and multitudes of other forms that later became extinct, some in Eurasia, some in North America, some in both places.

Despite all these comings and goings, as recently as a million years ago most of the best-known North American mammals of today—such as the bison, musk ox, elk, moose, mountain sheep, bear, wolf and others—still had not arrived in North America. And it might seem that they never could, for at that time their migration bridge lay beneath the waters, submerged by movements of the earth's crust. It did not sink very deep (most of it now lies from 45 to 300 feet below the Bering and Chukchi Seas), yet there is no geological evidence that the bridge has ever again been uplifted by further movements in the earth's crust. What did happen is that the sea level dropped far enough for the land bridge to emerge once again. This took place four times during the last million years, as huge ice sheets locked up much of the planet's water supply and lowered the level of all the oceans. Although there is some dispute about the exact depth to which the seas fell during the ice ages, a lowering of only 350 feet would have exposed a North Pacific land bridge as wide as present-day Alaska. One might think that since the greatest emergence of land was when the ice sheets were at their maximum, the bridge itself must have been covered by impassable ice too. But that is not so. Geological evidence reveals that, although the last glaciation extended down as far as Ohio, most of Alaska, as well as part of western Canada, was completely free of ice. Also at the very time that

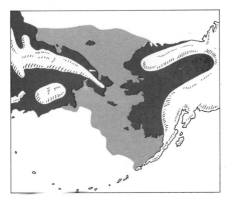

THE LAND BRIDGE FROM ASIA

At the height of the Wisconsin glaciation about 20,000 to 40,000 years ago, the level of the oceans was so low that a wide land connection existed between North America and Asia. It is shown here in color, with the present-day boundaries of Alaska and Siberia shown in gray. The great glaciers of the period (white with stippling) extended as far south as the present Midwest, but in Alaska they left enough room for plants and animals from Asia to become established, and—as the glaciers melted—to work their way deep into the continent. Glacial melt also caused the oceans to rise again and in time they covered the land bridge.

North America was most deeply locked in the icy grip, Siberia was only sparsely covered and may have served as a refuge for wildlife during this glacial advance. However, as the ice began to retreat from North America, ice-free corridors opened up, allowing migration of animals.

Thus, throughout much of the Pleistocene ice age—in fact until the most recent ice sheet began to melt about 12,000 years ago—a broad highway connected Eurasia and North America. It was probably relatively flat and covered in part by tundra or long-grass vegetation. The migrants that arrived in North America during the Pleistocene found a vast new world not much different in the conditions for life than the one they had left. In some cases, their ecological niches were already occupied and the new arrivals could not overcome the competition of established forms; these species never gained a foothold. In other cases the new arrivals found vacant niches—vacant because their earlier inhabitants had been extinguished, probably by the Pleistocene's drastic climate changes. Through isolation, radiation and natural selection, these successful invaders evolved into races and species that gradually became less and less like their relatives that remained in Eurasia. It is this process that explains the eerie likenesses but subtle differences that European explorers noticed when they first encountered the animals of North America.

But the fauna of North America that greeted the explorers is not accounted for solely by the bridge between Eurasia and Alaska. There was another land connection with yet another continent that also influenced the wildlife. Today North America is joined to South America by the funnel-shaped isthmus of Central America, which narrows to a mere thread of land at Panama. Throughout almost all of the Tertiary, however, until only a few million years ago, the southern boundary of North America was in Mexico. What now exists as Central America was then an archipelago of large islands. Today biogeographers draw the boundary of the Nearctic realm at approximately the isthmus of Tehuantepec, where the high Mexican plateau dips into lowland tropical forest, and south of which the first of these ancient islands probably began. During the tens of millions of years of the Tertiary when there was no Central American land bridge, the ancestors of a few animals such as the giant sloth apparently managed to reach North America by island hopping. But when movements of the earth's crust heaved up land connections between the two continents, a flood of animals began moving in both directions. This resulted in numerous duplications of types that had evolved separately on the two continents and filled the same ecological niches. These were now brought into direct competition, which resulted in the wholesale extinction of forms. Some survived, however—among the better-known South American invaders that still live in the Nearctic today are the porcupine and armadillo, the opossum, the curious horned toad and other iguanids, the hummingbirds, tanagers and tyrant flycatchers. Exactly what they replaced or exactly which niches they filled then we do not know.

I T would be an oversimplification to explain the fauna of North America that greeted the explorers simply in terms of these journeys across the land bridges from Eurasia and, to a lesser extent, from South America. For one thing, North America had also evolved its own animals, a few of which still survived. Some, like the pocket gopher, have never been found outside the continent. For still others the story was even more complicated, as demonstrated by the history of the opossum. Today the opossum is native to eastern and central North America, but the migrations of its ancestors, the didelphids, spanned three continents. Early in the Tertiary, they probably crossed from North America, their place of origin, to Eurasia and also to South America. Roughly 25 million years ago they disappeared from North America and Eurasia, but they continued to flourish in South America. Finally, after the two American continents became connected again several million years ago, the opossum was able to reinvade the northern continent.

A third complicating factor is that one must explain why certain animals crossed the land bridges but others failed to do so. Actually, land bridges act like filters. A complex interplay of changing climates around the bridges, ecological competition by similar animals and other factors all serve to keep out some species while admitting others. An example of the effect of ecological competition in the filter is the saiga antelope of Eurasia. It failed to become established presumably because its niche was already filled by an exclusively North American group of antelopelike animals, of which today's pronghorn of the plains is the only survivor. The cold climate at the Bering bridge probably filtered out numerous kinds of Eurasian mammals—Old World rats and mice, giraffes, mongooses, civet cats and higher nonhuman primates. There were also more subtle filtering factors at work. One type of rodent—squirrels—passed over the Bering land bridge, but another—prairie dogs—never left North America. No one knows for sure, but probable explanations are that prairie dogs met competition, are relatively sedentary and spread slowly, or found unsuitable soil conditions.

Thus, through the ebb and flow of migrations, through the diversification of successful migrants and the extinction of unsuccessful ones, North America came to be populated by the multiformity of wildlife that greeted the European explorers. It could not boast the varied marsupial life of Australia nor the variety of birds and monkeys of South America. But it did possess several distinctions. It was a crossroad along a great route of migration from the Old World to the American tropics; it was a cradle for the evolution of certain kinds of animals of its own; it was a place where during most of its history its wildlife developed free from the influence of man.

There is not a shred of evidence that *Homo sapiens* originated in the Americas or that he was preceded here by more primitive kinds of man. No fossils of primitive man—or of any primate more advanced than a premonkey—have ever been found in North America. All of man's near relations among the primates belong exclusively to the Old World. It is beyond doubt that *Homo sapiens* first arrived here as a recent immigrant from Asia. He spread out over North America, adapting his way of life to the animal and plant communities that had developed here. By the time the European explorers reached North America, they found a diversity of human cultures that ranged from exceedingly primitive hunting and gathering societies to high civilizations of agriculturalists that filled a wide range of ecological environments.

No sooner was the New World discovered than bizarre theories began to be conjured up to account for the presence of the Indians. One speculation was that they were children of Babel relegated to a primitive existence because of their sins. There was no shortage of other theories: Europe and America were believed to have been connected by the Lost Continent of Atlantis; the Indians were claimed as descendants of one of the Lost Tribes of Israel who had somehow reached the Americas; it was even believed that they might be descend-

THE MIGRATION CHRONICLES

It is well known that the Indians came to America via the Bering Strait, but most people are unaware that there is a document purporting to be a contemporary record of such a journey. This "Walam Olum," consisting of 183 pictographs accompanied by spoken verses passed from generation to generation, was discovered among the Delaware Indians in 1820. Though the original pictographs have disappeared, scholars who have devoted decades of intense study to the Walam Olum are convinced of its authenticity. Here some important verses dealing with the migration are quoted and keyed to a map, with a brief explanation of corresponding pictographs.

Crossing the Bering Strait

The northern and eastern divisions of the tribe decide "it would be good to live on the other side of the frozen water" (1). The triangles stand for land, the double line is ice, feathered circles are tribes. Previous verses tell a creation myth, complete with evil serpent and great flood.

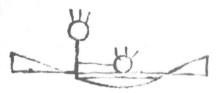

The great northern schism

Reaching what is now British Columbia, the tribes divide into factions (2). The rectangle represents land then occupied by the Delawares; the four tadpole-like glyphs are tribes leaving for the East—to become ancestors of a number of Canadian tribes, including the Cree (3), Ojibway (4) and Montagnais (5).

14

ants of Phoenicians or Carthaginians. But there is no longer any need for such ideas. Sufficient archeological evidence has emerged to make reliable inferences about the arrival of man on a virgin continent. He simply got here on his own two legs across dry land, before the melting of the last glacier caused the oceans to inundate the Bering Strait land bridge. The establishment of man in the New World probably occurred slightly less than 25,000 years ago, although there are some anthropologists who believe that this may have taken place as long ago as 40,000 years.

Much energy has been devoted in the past several decades to tracing the movements of these early arrivals—or Paleo-Indians, as they are often called—and now the trail is growing warm. It is impossible to be certain about their routes; nevertheless, a pattern is beginning to emerge. In recent years, about 750 prehistoric stone tools have been discovered at several sites at a pass in the Brooks Range of northern Alaska and along the Arctic coast of Yukon Territory, Canada. These tools are so distinctive in workmanship to the trained eye of the archeologist that it pays him to compare them with caches of similar tools found elsewhere. Such caches do, in fact, exist—clear across Asia and even into Europe. Their design and distribution reveal the possibility of spurts of human migration across Eurasia and deep into the interior of North America. Groups of tools found near Lake Baikal, Siberia, are considered by some authorities to be about 20,000 years old. This age fits in nicely with the optimum period for crossing the Bering land bridge, which was wide open from about 23,000 to 13,000 years ago. It seems probable that these people and the big-game herds they depended upon traveled northward across the foothills of the Siberian Arctic and then eastward across the land bridge and along the northern coast of Alaska. They could not immediately turn south because the high peaks of the Brooks Range formed a barrier parallel to the coast, but eventually they reached the Mackenzie River, the great north-flowing stream of Canada. Since it was ice-free at the time, they were undoubtedly able to work their way for a considerable distance inland up the Mackenzie River Valley. The movement of the Paleo-Indians was not a mass migration out of Asia, like that of the Mongol hordes which swept across Eurasia in historic times. Rather it seems to have consisted of a persistent trickle of generations of nomadic hunters who continued their Asiatic way of life in North America without ever being aware that they had invaded a vast new world.

THE fascinating part of all this is that humans may have made their way into North America even earlier. At present, such views are highly conjectural; however, animal fossils and tools have been discovered in Mexico which apparently date back 30,000 or 35,000 years. Where these first men in North America, possessors of primitive yet efficient tools, came from or who their descendants were is a total mystery. Whatever the case, they were able to fill an ecological vacuum and to harvest the abundant game of the continent. Obviously they did not pick and choose their routes to the interior of the continent. These Paleo-Indians followed the topography and the animal and plant life that was once again reclothing the continent as the ice retreated. By about 12,000 years ago the ice had melted sufficiently to open a corridor to the interior of the continent along the eastern flank of the Rocky Mountains. From the high plains east of the Rockies the Paleo-Indians flowed out in all directions—eastward to the woodlands and the Great Lakes, southeastward along the tributaries of the Mississippi River, westward through mountain passes to the

Great Basin and the Pacific coast. So persistent was the migration that these erstwhile Eurasians reached the southern tip of South America by at least 8,600 years ago, a distance of roughly 11,000 miles from their point of entry into the New World.

Man had arrived in the New World to stay. As the great ice sheet and the mountain glaciers melted, water poured back into the seas, the Bering land bridge was inundated and he was cut off from retreat. With the warming of the climate, the plant and animal life on the continent changed also: herds of large mammals dwindled and many kinds became extinct. To survive, most of the Indians had to adapt their technology to the changing environment, rather than remaining exclusively big-game hunters. They invented ingenious spear throwers and arrows for hunting smaller game; they developed pottery, irrigation works and horticulture. By the time of the European discovery of North America, they existed in 276 tribes, had worked out a bewildering variety of patterns of life and spoke more languages than are spoken in all of Europe.

THE major biomes that the Indians exploited were five in number. Across the northern roof of the continent is the treeless tundra, where the ground is permanently frozen a few feet below the surface and a profusion of flowering herbs, mosses, lichens and heaths clothe the soil in the brief summer growing season. During the summer, hordes of birds, particularly waterfowl, nest in the tundra, but most of them, except for a few like ptarmigans and snowy owls, desert it during the winter. The principal large mammals are musk oxen and caribou, preyed on by wolves, and sea mammals such as seals and walruses, preyed on by polar bears. The tundra is the most impoverished biome on the continent in the number of its resident species, yet Eskimos and Chipewyan Indians have managed to eke out a living from the caribou and sea mammals, supplemented by birds and fish.

Directly to the south of the tundra is the coniferous forest, extending unbroken across Canada from interior Alaska to the Atlantic Ocean. In its natural state, this vast green carpet is inhabited primarily by moose, caribou, black bears, wolves, lynxes, fishers and wolverines, as well as numerous kinds of songbirds that breed there during the summer. At the time of the European discovery, the coniferous forest was the home of various Athapascan and Algonquian Indian tribes, developers of the snowshoe, the birchbark canoe and the toboggan. They subsisted primarily on the meat of caribou and moose, as well as occasional bear, beaver and rabbit.

South of the coniferous forest lies the great deciduous-forest biome. The forest formerly covered most of the eastern United States between the St. Lawrence River and the Gulf of Mexico, and extended as far west as the prairies of Illinois and Texas. The deciduous forests grow where there is approximately 40 inches of rain a year and no sharply defined rainy or dry seasons. This was the biome whose bounty impressed the early explorers—a great diversity of trees, rich soil for agriculture, a wildlife that once included woodland bison, wolves, deer, mountain lions, martens, black bears and wild turkeys. Among the Indian tribes of this vast range were the eastern federation of the Iroquois nation and another group in the south known as the Five Civilized Tribes. They were largely sedentary and organized into far-flung political systems, relying upon an agriculture whose basic crops were corn, beans, pumpkins and tobacco. Unlike the Indians of the coniferous forest, for whom famine was an annual threat, they were able to fall back upon the bounty of the eastern forest

An era of agriculture

"When White Wildcat was chief there was much farming" says the ancient verse that accompanies this pictograph. Here, the "Cat Chief" stands next to a row of crops. This first mention of farming indicates that the tribe had moved south into rich agricultural country (6) and perhaps met other farming tribes.

An era of river travel

When "One Who Paddles" was chief, the Delaware tribes became more adventurous, leaving their farms to explore and travel on the rivers (7). A plausible explanation for this change is that land near villages was becoming less productive and stocks of game were depleted.

The migration reaches the ocean

As this pictograph indicates, the tribes eventually reached the Atlantic coast (8). By this time, a number of splinter factions had dropped out and established tribal nations that extended from the Rocky Mountains to the Atlantic Ocean.

Arrival of the first Europeans

The verse reports: " . . . persons floating in from the east: the Whites were coming." Scholars believe the visitor was John Cabot or Giovanni Da Verrazano; the date, therefore, is 1498 or 1524.

when crops failed. At such times they hunted deer, gathered nuts or caught fish.

In primeval America, the grassland extended from the eastern forests to the Rocky Mountains, from Alberta southward to about the Mexican border, covering the heartland of the continent with an immense inland sea of rippling grass. Its existence depended on irregular rainfall or on soil conditions that failed to provide a supply of water adequate for the growth of trees. In the pristine condition, the North American grassland swarmed with countless numbers of bison and pronghorns, hordes of rodents such as prairie dogs and pocket gophers, predators such as wolves, coyotes and mountain lions. The Plains Indians that inhabited the western grasslands are the "typical" American Indians known to every schoolboy. They wore feather bonnets, lived in cone-shaped tepees, hunted bison and—once they had obtained horses from the Spanish conquistadors—became superb riders. They included the Crow, Sioux, Cheyenne and Comanche tribes, some of the best known on the continent. The Prairie Indians (the Osage, Omaha, Illinois and Kansa) occupied the moister tall-grass prairie at the eastern end of the grasslands; they were bison hunters too, but they also farmed and lived in permanent villages part of the year.

Between the Rockies and the Sierra Nevada-Cascade mountains, extending southward to the Nearctic boundary in southern Mexico, is a vast arid region, marked by erratic precipitation combined with a high evaporation rate for the rain that does fall. Despite the scarcity of water and the daily extremes of temperature, the North American deserts harbored an amazing diversity of wildlife —mountain lions and bighorn sheep, javelinas, small mammals and a wealth of birds. In this biome lived the most primitive as well as the most culturally advanced Indians on the continent. The Great Basin tribes—among them Shoshonis, Paiutes and Utes—eked out a meager sustenance as gatherers of wild plants (piñon nuts, seeds and roots) or as hunters of pronghorns, rabbits, rodents, reptiles and insects. But to the south of these, in the deserts of Arizona, New Mexico and northern Mexico, other tribes developed a remarkable agriculture in oasislike places near streams. The Pueblo Indians dug elaborate networks of irrigation canals and built great cities on the bluffs and in the valleys. Still farther to the south, in Mexico proper, lay the high civilizations of the Aztecs and others. Their relatively huge numbers were sustained by intensive farming, domestication of dogs and turkeys for food, monumental irrigation works and well-organized totalitarian governments.

THESE were some of the patterns of life that had developed on the continent, and to the Indians they must have seemed as unalterable as its great mountain chains, dark woodlands, waving grasslands and sun-baked deserts. But when the new wave of migration spread over North America, arriving not across land bridges but across the sea from Europe, it changed the face of the continent, affected utterly every living thing on it and placed its stamp so quickly and drastically that it is beyond our power ever to restore even a semblance of the primeval lands. No one person ever knew the entirety of primeval America, for it was discovered piece by piece over several centuries. For us to obtain a picture of what America looked like when the earliest Europeans saw it, we must fit together ancient chronicles and records. This book is such a compilation—of the reports of the mammals and birds that were the original endowment of the continent, of the history of how some have vanished and many have become depleted, and finally of the efforts being made to preserve the vestiges of American wilderness that remain.

GULLS RIDE AN ICEBERG OFF THE ALASKAN COAST. THIS CHILL AND SOMBER NORTHERN LAND WAS EARLY MAN'S INTRODUCTION TO AMERICA

A New World Unveiled

The first human to see America was a primitive nomad wandering east out of Asia during the last ice age, when much of Siberia and Alaska was ice-free. From Alaska he and his kind slowly spread to all parts of the land—but they spread themselves thin, and Europeans, some 8,000 years later, found a continent still unspoiled. Even today, its brooding grandeur haunts the scenes they saw.

AN UNTAMED LAND DEFEATED SPAIN

The second great invasion of North America, which was to change forever the aspect of the continent, came from Europe—and Columbus gave Spain the jump on other nations. From the West Indies and Mexico, conquistadors marched north in search of gold. But single-minded as they were in their search for treasure, the immense natural riches of the land they saw meant little to them. To Coronado's men, the great southwestern deserts were only a barren, arid hell, the Grand Canyon a frustrating barrier whose river, unreachable far below, mocked them. Alarcón, cruising up the Gulf of California to support the Coronado expedition, likewise failed to realize the potential wealth that lay beyond the heat-shimmering coastline. Other Spaniards, pushing north and west from Florida, bogged down in great swamps, and though they found the Mississippi, never exploited it as a waterway. Defeated by the land, the Spaniards ironically enriched it with the priceless gift of horses, which the Indians seized upon.

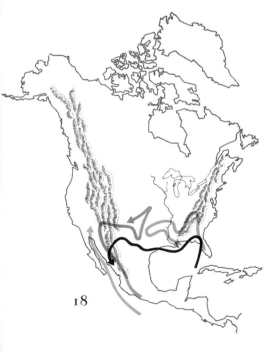

■ NARVAEZ AND
     CABEZA DE VACA—1528-1536
  DE SOTO—1539-1542
  CORONADO—1540-1542
  ALARCON—1540

THE GRAND CANYON IN WINTER

The snow in this picture would have been welcome to Don García López de Cárdenas, one of Coronado's men when, in 1540, he looked over the lip of the world's greatest canyon. It was summer in the desert then, and men and horses were parched, but try as they might, they found no way to reach the water they saw sparkling a mile below.

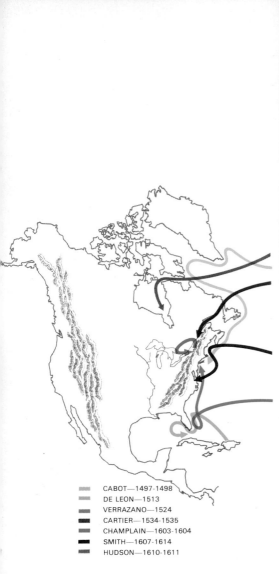

CABOT—1497-1498
DE LEON—1513
VERRAZANO—1524
CARTIER—1534-1535
CHAMPLAIN—1603-1604
SMITH—1607-1614
HUDSON—1610-1611

JAMESTOWN: LANDS TO SETTLE

Six years after Columbus, John Cabot, an Italian navigator in England's pay, had traversed the North Atlantic and established Britain's claims in the New World. The race was on. The French sent Cartier, who discovered the St. Lawrence River, giving France that valuable entry into the continent, while Verrazano charted much of the east coast for them. There were many more. The land those northern navigators found was far different from that the Spanish were exploring to the south. There were deep, brooding forests, full of game, a plenitude of streams and fertile valleys —in short, a land not to plunder, for there was no gold, but a land to settle. Jamestown, in Virginia, founded in 1607, was the first successful English colony. The pine grove at the right is thought to be the spot where Pocahontas begged her father to spare the life of John Smith, Jamestown's leading citizen.

20

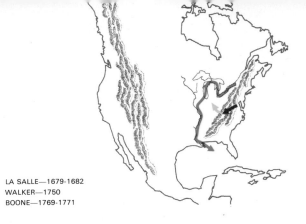

CUMBERLAND GAP: A WAY WEST

By the middle of the 17th Century, the exploitation of North America's natural wealth was drawing venturesome men of many nations to its shores—but the greatest prize, the immense heartland of the continent, still lay untouched, almost undreamed of. Spain claimed the lands along the Gulf coast but found her golden treasures to the south, in Mexico and Peru. English colonies dotted the Atlantic seaboard from the Carolinas to Maine, and the forests rang with the blows of their axmen. The Dutch in New Amsterdam were spreading out to farm the Hudson's fertile valleys, and France, pene-

trating through the St. Lawrence gateway, found wealth in the furs of beaver, marten, fox and bear in the deep north woods. The French came closest to realizing the enormous abundance of the New World which still lay undiscovered. La Salle, reaching the Illinois River, saw "vast meadows, with forests," spreading in every direction: "the soil," his men reported, "looks as if it had been already manur'd." Down the Mississippi he traveled, past some of the richest farmland men ever were to know; but he was looking for a water route to the Pacific, and he did not stay. The English, blocked by the rugged wall of the Appalachian range, made little effort to go farther inland than the fall line of the rivers. Thus, the tide of settlement lapped only at the coastline—until 1750, when Thomas Walker, surveying for a British company, found the Cumberland Gap, a natural breach in the Appalachian range. Then, Daniel Boone hacked out the 208-mile Wilderness Road into Kentucky, and now, as through a sluiceway, the tide flowed into the lush lands beyond. Today, protected as a National Historical Park, the Gap, viewed as it is here, differs little from what Boone and Walker saw.

BADLANDS, SOUTH DAKOTA

"Bad land for crossing," the Indians called this wild, eroded region. Here, where the White River and its tributaries have deeply etched the soft clay and sandstone, little has changed since the sons of the French fur trader Vérendrye, seeking a waterway west in 1742, first gazed on the Badlands. "Earths of different colors, as blue, a kind of crimson, grass-green, shining black, chalk white and ochre," was their description, and they found a surprising world of wildlife in the barren regions: rattlesnakes, mice and pack rats, badgers, coyotes and eagles nesting in the crags. But their search for a westward-leading river was in vain, as was that of Marquette and Joliet, who 69 years earlier had descended the Mississippi, supposing that it might flow into the Pacific. None of these men yet realized the vastness of the continent or even imagined the extent of the mountains which blocked the way. Nearly a century was to pass before trappers and pioneers mapped out the storied trails which ultimately opened the Far West.

24

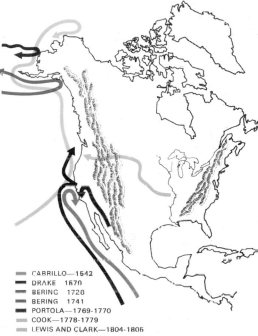

THE DISTANT PACIFIC SHORE

"There are mountains which seem to reach the heavens," reported Cabrillo's sailors, first to see the California coast. Later explorers, "delighted with the climate and the goodness of the soil," found fish and game plentiful and trees of "prodigious size." But so long as California was approached only by sea or from Mexico, the Spaniards were in the best position to settle the rich Far West, and they were slow to do so. Meanwhile, great herds of sea otter beckoned to fur traders from Russia, and settlers in the East grew restive at the tales brought back by trappers—of giant redwoods and valleys so rich that a man on horseback was hidden by tall grass. Belatedly the Spanish had sent Gaspar de Portolá north to establish garrisons at San Diego and Monterey. But only 35 years later, Lewis and Clark charted a way west overland, and soon a whole nation surged into the new lands. The upland creek at left flows into the Columbia in Oregon, along the route Lewis and Clark took out of the mountains to the Pacific.

27

2

The Crowded Coasts

THE shores of North America encompass ice floes, rocky headlands, forested coasts, sweeping sandy beaches, tropical mangrove islets—a richness of habitats and faunas unsurpassed by any other continent. Their common denominator is that in their primeval state they teemed with a tremendous richness and abundance of life. This they had until very recently—until Europeans began exploiting it. Now it is virtually gone and will never exist again.

Norse sagas reveal that Columbus' four voyages to the Americas were not the first made by Europeans: in the year 1000 A.D., Leif Ericson and 35 Vikings sailed south from Greenland. They reached a bleak land, probably Newfoundland, and then the wooded coast of Nova Scotia, which they named Markland, or "woodland." Continuing south, they reached a shore where "there was no want of salmon . . . larger salmon than they had before seen." They spent the winter but made no permanent settlement; the forest soon covered any trace of their visit. Their only lasting effect on the fauna of the continent may have been the accidental introduction of a small marine snail, a European periwinkle, now found along beaches as far south as New Jersey.

But the voyages of Columbus were different—they opened the way to the exploitation of the continent and marked the beginning of a precipitous decline in many kinds of American wildlife. Word of Columbus' "new-found islands" spread quickly through the seaports of Europe, and soon other ships were probing the boundaries of the New World. At first they retraced Columbus' path to the Caribbean and sailed through the maze of islands there. But later they fanned out and began creeping along the Gulf and Atlantic coasts, and eventually the Pacific too.

INFLUENCING much of the life of the Gulf and Atlantic shores as far north as Newfoundland are the warm waters of the northward-flowing current known as the Gulf Stream. Columbus encountered it in the Caribbean Sea and was so impressed by its powerful sweep that he decided it was responsible for the creation of the multitude of islands that speckle the Caribbean between North and South America: "I hold it for certain," he wrote, "that the waters . . . have thus carried away large tracts of land and that from here has resulted the great number of islands." A few years later, Ponce de León encountered the stream along the Florida coast and reported that "although they had great wind, they could not proceed forward, but backward." The Gulf Stream, we know today, is actually a portion of the great North Equatorial Current, which circles clockwise in the Atlantic Ocean between North America and Europe. This majestic wheeling of the Atlantic waters is set up by the rotation of the earth and by the prevailing winds that blow from the west in northern latitudes, and—nearer the equator, from the east—the trade winds. At a time when there was no continuous land connection between North and South America, much of the water that was being pushed westward by the trade winds undoubtedly flowed right by all the islands of the Caribbean out into the Pacific Ocean. But once Central America emerged as a continuous land mass, this was no longer possible. The water piling up at the narrow Yucatán Channel between Cuba and Mexico had to go somewhere, and it began flowing out into the Atlantic again through the Straits of Florida.

As it passes between Cuba and Florida on its way back to the Atlantic, the stream is of immense size—its width nearly a hundred miles, its depth a mile and its volume equal to several hundred Mississippi rivers. North of the Florida Keys, the stream lies close to the coast, its warm waters affecting the climate and allowing tropical vegetation to grow as far north as Palm Beach. The swirling eddies the stream sets up close to shore have also created the four most prominent capes of the South Atlantic coast: Cape Kennedy (formerly known as Canaveral), Cape Fear, Cape Lookout and Cape Hatteras. North of Hatteras, the stream leaves the borders of the continent and turns northeastward. Off the Grand Bank of Newfoundland, its deep blue waters are clearly distinguishable from the cold green waters of the southward-flowing Labrador Current. In fact, the Gulf Stream so maintains its identity even this far north that the bow of a ship, nosing into it, may for a moment be 20° warmer than the stern which is still in the Labrador Current.

The tropical wilderness that the Gulf Stream has created in southern Florida is unique in the United States. Although believed to have been sighted by Spaniards as early as 1502, the first positive record of it was made on Easter Sunday, 1513, when Ponce de León reported a coast of "wild green growth" abloom with flowers, which he named *Pascua Florida*, "Feast of Flowers." Soon he was coasting a maze of mangrove keys, which he called "Islands of the Martyrs" because the trees' contorted shapes reminded him of men writhing in agony. The trees were alive with birds, long-legged waders that are still the most spectacular wildlife inhabitants of this coast. The unsullied plumage of the great white heron and of the American and snowy egrets shines from the dark green of the mangrove foliage like a mirror. So many blue herons, ibises, wood storks and roseate spoonbills often overload a rookery that the treetops appear as if decorated for a Christmas pageant.

The magnificent birds of the Keys have been hard pressed by the heavy hand of man. At one time or another, most of them have been in danger of extinction, and some are still exceedingly rare. At the end of the last century, immense numbers of them were being slaughtered to satisfy the prevailing women's fashion for feathered hats. The magnitude of this destruction can be judged from the fact that, during only one nesting season, a single feather merchant of the many operating in Jacksonville shipped 130,000 bird skins to the New York millinery market. The slaughter took place at the nesting time, since that is when the birds come into their finest plumage, which meant that the killing of the adults brought death to many times that number of young birds as well. It was a gruesome business, and public disgust eventually led to the formation of organizations to combat it. One of these, the parent of today's National Audubon Society, succeeded in 1901 in getting a bill enacted which is still the basis for bird protection in Florida. Wardens were hired by the organizations to enforce the new law. But the poachers were tough, resisted controls, and they murdered one of the first four Audubon men stationed in Florida. Nevertheless, the Society kept up the fight and was later joined by the State of Florida. This work has actually saved several species. The American and snowy egrets have leaped back spectacularly from the borderline of extinction. The roseate spoonbill, which was virtually extirpated from North America, is now out of danger. Unfortunately, many of these bird species are again being threatened—this time indirectly. The Florida building boom is depriving them of feeding and nesting areas except in Everglades National Park and other smaller sanctuaries.

THE most isolated islands in the chain of Keys that trails southwestward from the tip of Florida are the Tortugas (turtles), some 60 miles west of Key West, so named by Ponce de León for the huge numbers of green turtles that covered the islands at egg-laying time. The green turtle no longer breeds in the Tortugas, or anywhere else in North America for that matter, although once it ranged all along the Atlantic coast as far north as Massachusetts and was so abundant that a single hunter might catch a hundred in a day. Pursued for its meat and for its eggs, it was one of the first species in North America to be decimated by man. Although the islands' namesake is no longer present, the Tortugas are still notable as the only breeding place in North America for several kinds of tropical birds, particularly the sooty and noddy terns. So abundant are the sooty terns that a visitor must tread carefully to find a path through their closely packed nests. Living in as close quarters as they do, the sooty terns have to depend on complex behavioral adaptations to keep them from crowding each other out and yet to avoid constant and damaging fighting among themselves. They do this by squawking, flapping their wings and alternately flaring up and quieting down, each tern maintaining a necessary minimum of space around its own nest. They have no defense against man, however. Audubon visited the Tortugas in 1832 and found a party of Spanish eggers there, busily removing eight tons of tern eggs. This kind of exploitation reduced the nesting population to about 7,000 sooty and only 200 noddy couples by the end of the

19th Century. Today, under protection of the National Park Service, the number of sooty terns is back to around 80,000.

Of all the unusual forms of wildlife that the explorers found on the tropical coast of the continent, none was so strange as the sea mammal known as the manatee, which appeared to give credence to ancient legends of mermaids and sirens. In the early years of exploration, the manatee was common on the Gulf coast, in the West Indies and on the Atlantic coast occasionally as far north as North Carolina. The manatee possesses only one feature that might form the basis for the mermaid legend: its prominent breasts. Otherwise, it is a sluggish and uncomely animal, a ponderous browser on underwater vegetation. Its face is wrinkled and bristled, its skin rough; its body length ranges between nine and 15 feet, and it weighs between 600 and 2,000 pounds. No doubt there was disillusion as soon as the manatees were examined closely. Columbus "saw three sirens which came up very high out of the sea, but they were not as beautiful as they are painted, and in some ways they are formed like a man in the face." Science has paid homage to the sailors' illusions about sirens by classifying them, along with the related dugongs of the Old World, in the order Sirenia.

The Spanish explorers quickly turned to the manatee as a source of fresh meat, and so did the pirates that later cruised the Spanish Main and found secret anchoring places in the maze of lagoons where manatees lived. The now-extinct Timucuan Indians of Florida harpooned them from canoes; the Seminoles preyed upon them until driven into the interior by the Spaniards; in the last century, American fishermen killed them recklessly for meat and for sport. By 1895, the manatee had almost disappeared. But a few persisted in the inaccessible Everglades, and a Florida law passed in 1907 now protects them. They are no longer regarded as rare in southern Florida, but they are still absent from most of the coastal areas where they lived in primeval America.

WHILE the Spaniards were exploring the southernmost boundaries of the continent, ships from other nations were putting in all along the Atlantic shore. In 1524, Giovanni da Verrazano, an Italian captain sent to claim land in the name of France, made a landfall to the south of Cape Fear, near present-day Wilmington, North Carolina. He was particularly impressed by the extensive sand dunes—"the spacious land, so high that it exceeds the sandy shore . . . full of the largest forests, some thin and some dense, clothed with various sorts of trees, with as much beauty and delectable appearance as it would be possible to express." The coastal dunes of the southern states must have been a magnificent sight to behold in their untouched splendor, but today most of them have been leveled to make way for shorefront cottages and developments. Nevertheless, at a few places—notably Cape Hatteras National Seashore—the dunes have been preserved; dune grass, loblolly pine and dwarf oak can still be seen holding down the shifting grains of sand.

Continuing northward, Verrazano discovered Chesapeake Bay, which he thought was a strait that might lead to the riches of China and India. Eighty-five years before the arrival of Henry Hudson, he sailed into New York bay: "a very pleasant place situated among certain little steep hills through which there ran to the sea an exceedingly great stream of water," the river later to be named after Hudson. Still steering a northward course, he reached the Maine coast, where he was impressed, as people still are today, by its contrast with the South Atlantic shore: "We found it to be another land, high and full of thick woods of firs and cypresses such as are wont to grow in cold countries."

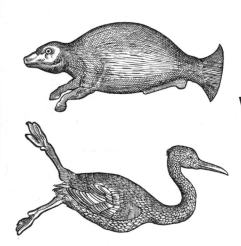

SOME PRETTY FANCY ANIMALS

Ancient America was a place of fabulous creatures in the eyes of Europeans, thanks to tales and drawings based on the testimonies of early explorers. The two sketches on this page, by a 17th Century Spaniard, were supposed to represent a manatee and a merganser duck. But the manatee was given a pointed snout, hoofs on its front flippers and the fantail of a fish. The bird, scrupulously labeled Mergus Americanus, appears to have the head of a merganser but the feet and tail of a grebe and the neck of an anhinga. A picture of beavers as busy as people (opposite), which appeared in the next century, was also commonly accepted as real.

Strangely, Verrazano failed to mention Cape Cod, where he would have found dunes that surpassed even those of the South Atlantic; indeed, Cape Cod was not discovered until 1602, despite the fact that it thrusts its prominent arm far into the Atlantic. The first landfall at Cape Cod was made by the Pilgrims in 1620, and the history of their colony records their reaction: ". . . what could they see but a hideous wilderness, full of wild beasts and wild men? . . . the whole country, full of woods and thickets, represented a wild and savage hue." Now, almost 350 years later, the "hideous wilderness" is forever gone, its woods cut and burned, the wild beasts and Indians extirpated. The towering dunes, however, have endured. When Henry David Thoreau trod their wind-swept solitude during the middle of the last century, he anticipated that this shore would someday be subjected to human development, although he could not possibly have envisioned the gasoline stations, motels and eateries that exist today. He remarked dryly that even with the advent of cottages, "this shore will never be more attractive than it is now."

THE remnants of the huge dunes and marshes along the Great Beach of Cape Cod—the place of which Thoreau said "a man may stand there and put all America behind him"—were belatedly set aside as the National Seashore Park in 1961. Missing from this landscape today are not only the beasts and the virgin woods but also the heath hen, a subspecies of the western prairie chicken, which once ranged from Massachusetts to the Potomac River. At the beginning of the 19th Century, the heath hen had been "so common on the ancient brushy site of Boston, that . . . servants stipulated with their employers not to have Heath Hen brought to the table oftener than a few times a week." But this plenty did not last, for by 1855 only one bird was found on the Massachusetts mainland and that last one was killed on Cape Cod. By 1877, the heath hen existed solely on Martha's Vineyard, an island off Cape Cod, where only about 200 birds survived; this number fell to a mere 60 in 1908. A sanctuary was established and a last ditch attempt made to save the heath hen. Under rigorous protection, the population increased to about 2,000 by 1916—but brush fires, disease and, in the end, too few breeding females reduced the population to the single individual which lived until 1932.

Impressed as Verrazano and other explorers of the North Atlantic coast were by the woodlands, dunes and bird life, nothing astonished them so much as the waters teeming with fish. Close to shore, there were young herring and cod and, at the mouths of rivers, great sturgeon between six and nine feet in length. An early account of the sturgeon reported that there was "an abundance of great fish leaping about the water on each side of us as we sailed," but no one sees these huge sturgeon off the New England shore today. The prime fishery resource was the cod, which were caught "so fast as the hook came down"; John Cabot stated that they were so thick they could be hauled out of the sea in baskets. Undoubtedly the Norsemen had discovered the cod fisheries of the North Atlantic about 1000 A.D.; by the early 17th Century, vessels from England, France, Spain and Portugal were harvesting the cod. The explanation for the impressive numbers of huge cod is to be found in the cold waters of the Labrador Current that sweep southward down the Atlantic coast as far as Cape Cod. The current carries with it certain salts, particularly phosphates and nitrates, needed by plants for growth, and the combination of cold water and salts creates ideal growing conditions for microscopic free-floating plants known as diatoms. These flourish to such an extent off Cape Cod that they are estimated to num-

THE LEGENDARY BEAVERS

What impressed the early French explorers about beavers was the fact that they built dams—and so it is not very surprising that an early 18th Century French map of North America should show them doing just that. Furthermore, the beavers are mixing mortar, carrying it to the dam on their tails and turning out a product worthy of an engineer.

ber as many as 400 million per cubic yard of water. The diatoms serve as a luxuriant pasture for the tiny Crustacea, particularly copepods and shrimps, that feed upon them. The copepods, in turn, are fed upon by young herring. That is where the cod enter the picture—they eat the herring.

The cod fisheries quickly became an important food source for Europe, and some of the early settlers along the New England coast made fortunes from them. But other forms of life—sea birds—had based their economy on the abundant fish long before. Jacques Cartier's first sight of the New World in 1534 was a rocky island off Newfoundland aswarm with such numbers of sea birds that "all the ships of France might load a cargo of them without once perceiving that any had been removed." And as Cartier cruised southward along the Newfoundland coast, he came upon other islets, including the noted Bird Rocks, that were "as completely covered with birds, which nest there, as a field is covered with grass."

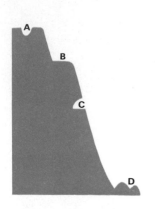

THE AUKS' APARTMENT HOUSES

On seaside cliffs and offshore islands from Maine to Labrador, millions of sea birds nest each spring in what seems a millionfold confusion of beating wings and squalling cries. But there is a basic order here, determined by nesting sites. The family of auks, or alcids, for instance, divides available dwellings on a cliff (above) between four of its species. The topmost site (A) is occupied by puffins (opposite), which build crude nests in burrows dug in the ground. Murres lay their eggs on the bare rock of a ledge (B); a tapered shape helps keep the eggs from rolling off. The razor-billed auk chooses the shelter of a crevice or overhang (C), and the black guillemot finds a bed of pebbles or shells, concealed under crevices or loose rocks at the bottom (D). The black guillemot lays two eggs; all the others just one, though the murre will replace a lost egg.

THE bird islands from St. Lawrence Bay to Newfoundland were the scene of perhaps the first systematic destruction of a North American wildlife resource. While conquistadors and explorers were seeking gold and a passageway to the Indies, humble European fishermen who left no chronicles of exploits had already discovered the bird colonies of the alcid family (auks, puffins, guillemots and murres), and gannets, kittiwakes and other gulls. It soon became habitual for the fishing craft to lay in stores of salted birds and fresh eggs, and the sea bird colonies went into rapid decline. Only the inaccessibility of some of the rocky islands and the precariousness of the breeding ledges allowed these birds to hold out as long as they did. An approximation of the sight that greeted these sailors can be seen today at Bonaventure Island, off Quebec's Gaspé Peninsula. There, cliffs hundreds of feet high are crammed, during late spring and summer, with all the species of sea birds seen by the explorers except the great auk and the Labrador duck, both of which are now extinct.

Little is known about the Labrador duck, except that it is known to have been hunted by European man; the last birds probably survived until about 1875. Much more is known about the extinction of the great auk, the "penguin" of the North Atlantic, a large flightless bird that once bred on rocky ledges and islands along much of the coast. The greatest known auk breeding colony was on Funk Island off the coast of Newfoundland. The birds there were steadily plundered by mariners as far back as the 16th Century, and as late as the Revolutionary War it was still profitable to go there despite the hazards of steep rocks and heavy surf, for the auks supplied meat, feathers and eggs. Later their bodies were rendered down for oil. When a naturalist visited Funk Island in 1841 he found nothing but heaps of bones.

The great auk was probably the first North American bird species to become extinct because of Western man. It was particularly vulnerable, not only because of its inability to fly but also because it had little fear of man. It was a rare bird as early as 1800 and finally became extinct in 1844 when the last two surviving birds were killed and their single egg smashed off the coast of Iceland.

Although today diminished numbers of birds of the North Atlantic coast still survive, the sea mammals have not fared so well. The sea mink was mentioned in early narratives, but little is known about it and it became extinct about 1860. It once ranged southward from Newfoundland to Massachusetts, but no drawings from life exist and all that remain to mark its life on the planet are a single stuffed specimen in a private collection and some bones and two pieces of skin discovered in the excavations of Indian village sites. Walruses and whales, although both mentioned by Cartier as common in northeastern waters, no longer are. The walruses, butchered for their ivory and blubber, disappeared from the American colonies in 1734 and today are found only in the cold seas of Alaska, northern Canada and Greenland.

Certain whales are as good as gone. The early populations of alongshore whales—those that stayed close to the land as opposed to species that kept to the open oceans—would be unbelievable to people familiar with the New England coast today. "Every day we saw whales plying hard by us," wrote a passenger when the *Mayflower* was anchored off Plymouth in 1620. A mariner sailing down east in 1635 reported that he saw "mighty whales spewing up water in the air like the smoke of a chimney." These were undoubtedly Atlantic right whales, a species that abounded along the North Atlantic coast, moving south to the Carolinas during the winter. It got its name from being the "right" whale to catch—it floated when harpooned instead of sinking.

At first the colonists harvested only stranded whales, as the Indians had done. But by 1672 the people of Nantucket were hunting the alongshore whales by boat—first by large rowboat manned by several oarsmen and a harpooner, later by seagoing vessels that could keep after the whales for days or weeks at a time until a full cargo had been obtained. The Nantucketers were extremely successful, and soon there were other whaling ports at Salem, Edgartown and New Bedford, all in Massachusetts, and in Sag Harbor, Long Island. Alongshore whaling reached its peak in 1726 when 86 whales were taken by ships out of Nantucket alone. But the resource had been overexploited; in 1727 a Boston newspaper stated: "we hear from the Towne of the Cape that the Whale-Fishery among them had failed much this Winter, as it has done for several Winters past." The decline in shore whales, together with the discovery of schools of sperm whales in the Atlantic, widened the arena to the open seas and eventually to all the oceans of the world. But the story of the relentless hunt for the earth's whales lies outside the scope of a chapter about North America's shores. The right whale, the only alongshore whale on the Atlantic coast, was decimated in a scant 50 years; it was virtually extinct by the time the International Whaling Convention of 1937 belatedly attempted to preserve the planet's diminished whale resource. Today it is making a feeble recovery; a "pod"—a school—is sometimes now seen off Cape Cod by fishermen.

Although the Gulf and the Atlantic coasts were the scenes of the first intrusions by European man upon the wildlife of the North American continent, it was not long before explorers were investigating the Pacific coast. Francis Drake, privateering in the Pacific in 1579, was probably the first person to report on the fogs of the San Francisco region: "neither for 14 days could they see the sun for the fogginess of the air." Several factors have conspired to produce the great fogs that lie along the Pacific coast from northern California to Alaska during the spring and summer. At this period of the year, there is a strong southward-flowing current of cold water along the coast. It is met by winds blowing inland from the Pacific; these have traveled across thousands of miles of ocean and have accumulated great quantities of moisture. When these winds come into contact with the air above the cold currents, they are cooled suddenly. The moisture they carry condenses, in much the same way that droplets collect on the outside of a glass of ice water. The droplets of water attach themselves to particles of salt thrown up by the spray, creating a haze which soon thickens

PUFFINS

MURRES

RAZOR-BILLED AUK

BLACK GUILLEMOT

into fog. The fogs are blown inland through gaps in the coastal mountain ranges. They are a substitute for rainfall, which is rare during the summer months along the coast; the droplets of fog collect on the branches of trees and eventually fall to the ground where they maintain the moisture of the soil.

Wherever this fog belt exists north of the Monterey peninsula in California, it allows the tallest trees on earth to grow, the coast redwoods. In fact, redwoods are rarely found farther inland than the fog pockets, and the very existence of a stand of them is proof that sea fogs penetrate inland at that place. Strangely enough, it was not until 1769 that the redwoods were first seen by Spanish explorers; they were baffled by the sight of "some tall trees of reddish-colored wood of a species unknown to us, having leaves very unlike those of the cedar, and without a cedar odor; and as we know not the names of the trees, we gave them that of the color of the wood, *palo colorado*." The huge size of the *palo colorado*, or "redwood," amazed the Spaniards—they reported that eight men holding hands could not form a circle around the base of one. When it was later discovered that they were valuable timber, their destruction began apace. Many organizations and individuals fought to save them, and none was more energetic than John Muir, the young Scot who explored the western wilderness and foresaw the threat to these trees. "No doubt these trees would make good lumber after passing through a sawmill," he wrote, "just as George Washington after passing through the hands of a French cook would have made good food." The Muir Woods, a grove of redwoods preserved north of San Francisco, are named in his honor. But cutting continues even today. A mere quarter of the original stand remains and the U.S. Forest Service has warned that, at the present rate of cutting, almost all of it will be gone by 1980. Even the pitifully small remnants set aside in state parks—75,000 acres—are threatened by highways planned to slice through their quiet groves.

Gold-hungry Spaniards had sailed the Pacific coast as early as 1542; they had made overland treks across California and, ironically, passed within scant miles of the richest gold source on the continent. They overlooked not only the gold but also another source of riches. As early as 1741, the Russian explorer Vitus Bering had reached the northern Pacific shores from Siberia. But little or no attention was paid to his explorations until his ship returned from its second voyage—loaded with a thousand skins of sea otters. An international stampede then began to gather the furs; probably the most beautiful in the world—shining silky black, unbelievably soft and thick. A single cargo was sometimes worth a million dollars.

The sea otter weighs up to 80 pounds, about four times as much as the inland otter of streams and lakes. It spends almost its entire life in the water, never feeding on land but instead diving for snails, mussels and crustaceans that live on the sea bottom near shore. To break their hard shells, the sea otter lies on its back in the water and smashes them on a rock which it holds on its chest. Much of the life of the sea otter centers around the kelp beds, tremendously long seaweeds that float close to shore. The otters sleep floating on their backs in the kelp, wrapping a few strands around themselves as anchors. They use the kelp as a breakwater against waves, and they find sanctuary in the beds from killer whales that prowl the coast. As soon as the young otter is two days old the mother moors it to a frond of kelp while she goes off to hunt in the depths. Its usual method of locomotion when not in a hurry is to swim on its back, propelling itself by alternate strokes of its webbed hind feet.

Sea otters have been described as being as frolicsome as the inland otters, and mild-tempered and attentive parents. But these traits, so admired in humans, did not protect them against human depredations. On the contrary, they were characteristics that humans exploited. Hunters soon learned that the females are particularly solicitous of their young. To capture an adult female, all they had to do was locate and kill a young one; this would entice the mother within range. The slaughter that took place around the Pribilof Islands of Alaska was typical of what happened all along the coast. On a single island in the Pribilofs more than 5,000 otters were killed the first year they were hunted; the following year a thousand skins were obtained; the seventh year none—the sea otter was extinct on that island. Throughout their range, extending in a sweeping arc across the northern Pacific from southern Japan to lower California, they were pursued relentlessly, becoming so rare that the entire year's take in 1900 was only 127 skins. In 1910, the last legal otter pelt was marketed—for a price of $1,703.33. An international treaty the next year afforded protection to the otter —but only a handful of them remained to be protected.

In the 50 years since then, the otter has made a slow comeback. The estimate of the Alaskan population at present is between 20,000 and 30,000 animals. Farther south, the otter was believed totally extinct until a small herd of 94 was discovered in 1938 near Monterey, California. Stringently protected, they too have increased and now number about 1,000 animals in small bands along the rocky coast between Point Lobos and the Santa Barbara Islands of California. But the prospect that the otters will repopulate their former range outside of Alaska appears bleak. Increased building all along the coast is already limiting the few places where they can live and breed undisturbed. But the greatest hazard is presented by oil slicks from coastal ships. So soft and delicate is the otter's fur that only a small amount of oil floating on the surface will gum it up and destroy its insulating properties. This is fatal to the otter, for fur is its sole protection against cold water; unlike other sea mammals, it lacks a blubber layer.

The Pacific shore is the home of a wide variety of other kinds of sea mammals—fur seals, harbor seals, the California sea lion (the trained "seal" of the circus) and the huge Steller sea lion. All these belong to a group of exclusively marine mammals known as the pinnipeds and classified within the order Carnivora. They are set apart from other carnivores in that they are strikingly modified for life in the water. Their limbs are flippers—the rear ones wide and paddlelike, the front ones usually tapered. Their behavior in the water is fishlike—they swim and steer with their flippers and body, and catch food directly in the mouth. Despite their marine adaptations, the pinnipeds are still linked to the land—all must return to a solid surface, whether it be a rock or an ice raft, to give birth, and in some species the pups are not born swimmers but must learn how.

O F all the pinnipeds of North America, only the northern fur seal rivals the sea otter in the persecution by man it has withstood. When Gerasim Pribilof, a navigator for a Russian trading company, in 1786 discovered the five barren volcanic islands named for him in the Bering Sea, the total population of northern fur seals is believed to have been at least five million. Each summer the seals return to these treeless and fogbound islands to breed; during the rest of the year, their small bands are found as far south as Baja California, following the schools of fish on which they feed. How many seals were killed in the Pribilofs will never be known. The figure is surely a huge one, for more than two million were slaughtered in only 40 years between 1867 and 1907. Four years later

THE DEXTEROUS SEA OTTER

In its typical feeding position (above), a sea otter sculls along on its back with one foot or the other as it cracks with a rock the shellfish on which it feeds. Then, tucking the rock into a pocketlike fold of skin under its arm (in which it also often keeps a supply of extra food), it will turn and, in a single, splashless motion, dive to the bottom for more. Otters have been seen playing with rocks and shells, throwing them from one paw to another for hours at a time. Mothers shelter their young on their chests; if they have to leave the pups for any length of time, they may wrap them in a kelp strand to keep them from drifting away. And though an otter is large at birth—five to six pounds—it receives maternal care until it is three or four years old, by which time, like its parents, it can dive 100 feet or more.

an international treaty protecting the fur seal was agreed upon—none too soon, for a mere 124,000 animals remained. Their recovery, however, has been dramatic since then—one of the outstanding examples on the continent of a successful effort to restore an animal species. The seal herd now totals over three million animals, despite controlled hunting to avoid overcrowding. The kill each year of about 65,000 fur seals is valued at about five million dollars—two thirds the total price paid to the Russians for all of Alaska. So crowded are the islands once again with fur seals that they probably represent the greatest concentration of mammalian life at any one place on earth. Unfortunately, the related Guadalupe fur seal of southern California and Mexico has not fared so well. It was believed extinct at the beginning of this century, but lone bulls were sighted in 1949 and 1951; in 1954 a band of 14 was found on Guadalupe Island, off Mexico's west coast, and there are now more than 200 there.

The northern fur seal symbolizes the destruction—and ultimate restoration—of one pinniped, but other species have not been so fortunate. The Steller or northern sea lion, for example, remains unprotected, and its numbers are diminishing steadily throughout its range between Alaska and California. Only in Alaska is it making a strong stand, and there the salmon fishermen regard it as a competitor for the reduced numbers of salmon in these waters, although the real salmon shortage is caused by overfishing by humans and the construction of dams. Similarly, the California sea lion once ranged from Puget Sound all the way to Mexico, but in the middle of the last century it was pursued so persistently that its vast herds were reduced to only a few thousand individuals. Even today these animals find no relief from persecution. Commercial and sport fishermen continue to condemn sea lions unjustly for consuming great quantities of fish, despite the evidence of one recent year which indicated that the sea lion in California waters ate about 18 million pounds of fish while commercial fishermen were taking 801 million pounds. Some years ago, two young Steller sea lions were shot by commercial fishermen because they appeared to be feeding on the salmon leaping all around them. When their stomach contents were examined, it was discovered that they had not fed on a single salmon. Instead, they had been eating lampreys—one of the most destructive enemies of the salmon.

M OST explorers who coasted the fringes of North America were content to remain offshore, making only brief forays inland or anchoring at island outposts for food and fresh water. The continent's great mountains and dark forest barriers loomed forbidding and mysterious to these seekers of the passage to the riches of the Indies. On the Atlantic coast, until the settlement of Virginia more than a hundred years after the discovery of the New World, no explorer except Verrazano penetrated more than five miles inland, and he only in Rhode Island. And of all the early explorers, probably only Amerigo Vespucci had the insight to realize that this new land was neither the shores of China nor a large island, but a huge new continent which he described as "more populous and full of animals than our Europe or Asia or Africa, and even more temperate and pleasant." However, the exploration of the virgin continent was not begun, as might have been expected, by the mariners of the coastal waters, who so easily could have penetrated the interior by entering the numerous bays and navigable rivers. Rather, the land life of the continent was first seen in all of its variety and abundance from the direction one might least expect. Spaniards, their armor clinking, marched northward from Mexico across the pitiless heat of the desert and from Florida through the dark swamps.

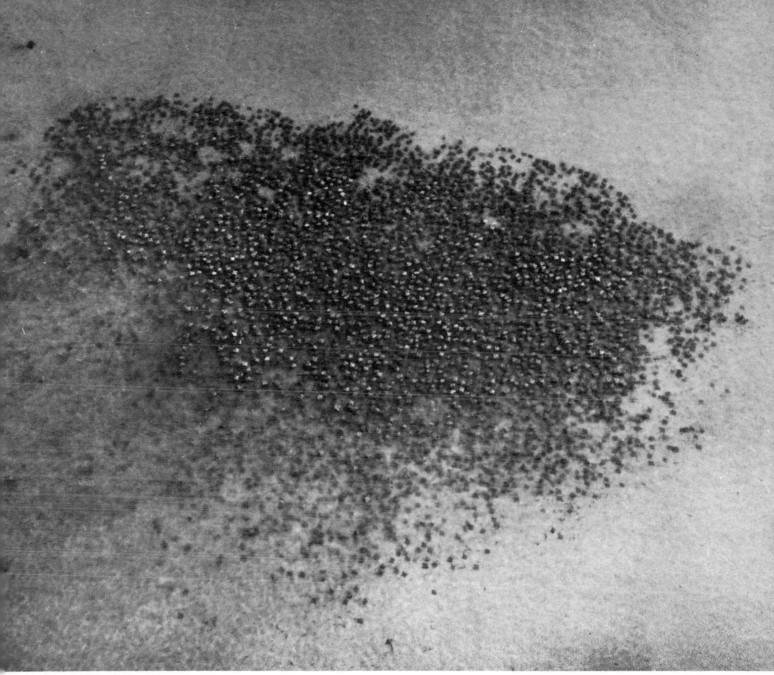

THOUSANDS OF COWNOSE RAYS, IN A RARE AND INEXPLICABLE MASS ACTION, PACK TOGETHER IN SHALLOW WATERS OFF SARASOTA, FLORIDA

Bounty at Land's End

From the ice-locked Arctic to the subtropics, the shores of North America harbor a staggering abundance of coastal life. Scores of species of sea birds breed in marshland, beach and rockbound habitats, and there are fish in such profusion that entire economies have been based upon them. Hidden in the sands, insects in their own world have built communities of extraordinary intricacy.

The Sandy Shores

Ever since the geological birth of North America, the seas have been breaking down coastal rocks to build, along with sediment from rivers, an almost unbroken chain of beaches from Mexico to northern California and from Florida to New England. Jutting out like a giant sickle, Cape Cod marks the northern boundary of the great sandy beaches of the Atlantic coast—but the Cape is itself a geological oddity, shaped by glaciers that deposited billions of tons of debris along the Massachusetts coast. Spared some of the human abuses that have destroyed so many of North America's beaches, Cape Cod is still a major stopover point for numbers of migratory birds, although egg hunters in the last century nearly expunged the local bird population. In 1961 the Cape was belatedly set aside as a National Seashore and hopefully will remain as one of the last outposts of wilderness along the crowded eastern coast.

THE LONELY DUNES of Cape Cod are exposed to the full fury of North Atlantic weather, and tides and winter storms so buffet its beaches that the shoreline is constantly being changed.

A LAUGHING GULL, FLYING IN SEARCH OF FOOD, NEARLY SOMERSAULTS AS IT SNATCHES A MORSEL FROM THE WATER. ALL SEA GULLS ARE

A YEARLY VISITOR to Cape Cod, the three-toed sanderling breeds in the Arctic and migrates deep into the Southern Hemisphere. It has long mystified ornithologists with its uncanny capacity for instantaneous communication: every member of a huge flight can change direction in mid-air simultaneously, as if on signal, although there is no apparent leader.

SUPERB AERONAUTS, ABLE TO SOAR ALONG COASTAL UPDRAFTS FOR HOURS, ALTHOUGH THEY PREFER A FISH DIET, THEY EAT ALMOST ANYTHING

THE MAINE COAST exemplifies the stark beauty of the North Atlantic shore. From these waters men have long reaped a seafood bounty, as shown below by racks of pickled alewives.

The Rugged Rocks

In the northern reaches of both the Pacific and Atlantic coasts, where the mountains meet the sea, the last vestiges of a hospitable shoreline vanish. Icy rivers plunge into the ocean; beaches are at best tiny pockets among the surf-lashed rocks. Each spring along the east coast enormous schools of alewives—small and bony but tasty members of the herring family—enter the wild waters and fight their way upstream to spawn. Certain pools and bottlenecks become so congested that a fisherman with a dip net can catch as many as he has strength to scoop up—sometimes as many as 100 barrels a day.

43

ALEWIVES JAM A POOL IN MAINE'S DAMARISCOTTA RIVER

PLACID AS THEY SEEM, CALIFORNIA'S ANTIOCH DUNES HARBOR A SWARMING AND VORACIOUS INSECT WORLD ON AND BENEATH THEIR SANDS

A Remarkable Insect Metropolis

The complexity of insect communities is nowhere better illustrated than on the Antioch dunes of northern California, near San Francisco. This colony is of such scope and diversity that it has attracted entomologists from all around the world. On this and the following pages, Walter Linsenmaier shows in minute detail what has been discovered here by scientists who have devoted decades to studying the dunes. His paintings reveal a complex world in which every insect in the community fills a specific ecological role as predator, prey or parasite in an endless interplay of life and death. Some, like the replete ants, exist only as passive food reservoirs for their fellows. Others, like the two types of aphids, feed directly on vegetation and are thus the first animal link in a long food chain which ends with such fierce predators as the robber fly or the parasitic cuckoo wasp. But perhaps most remarkable is the fact that this crowded, complicated and fiercely competitive world continues to exist year after year in a state of perfect balance, governed and motivated by the forces of instinct alone.

DAMSELFLY

MINING BEE

HONEY ANT

CUCKOO BEE

HONEY ANT

ANT LION LARVA

HONEY ANT COLONY

HISTER BEETLE

THE BUSTLING LIFE beneath the sands of the Antioch dunes includes a colony of *honey ants (lower left)* which feeds on nectar from nearby lupine plants or honeydew milked from other insects. In their burrow *(bottom level)*, they regurgitate nectar into worker ants of their own species, called *repletes*, that are specifically adapted to serve as receptacles for storing food. In the gallery above them are eggs tended by *nurse ants*, and to the right is the *queen*, her abdomen swollen with eggs. Nearby, an *ant lion larva* seizes a honey ant that has slid down into its conical trap. Below it a predatory *hister beetle* lumbers along, virtually immune to attack in its heavy armor. The *blue damselfly* at upper left carries a parasitic red *water mite* on its side. A *mining bee*, one of the many species which stocks its burrow with honey-filled pots, is followed by a *cuckoo bee:* this parasite will lay its own eggs in the mining bee's pots, and when they hatch, the cuckoo bee larvae will feed on the honey store.

BLISTER BEETLES

HOVER FLY

APHID WASP

ROBBER FLY

HOVER FLY LARVA

SAND WASP

GIANT COTTON BEE

LUPINE APHID

FOUR-SPIN CUCKOO W

Swarming over a purple-flowered lupine plant, tiny green *lupine aphids* drink nectar from the stem. The aphids are sometimes milked for this sweet food by honey ants *(previous page)* but are more often eaten by predators like the *hover fly larva*, which may consume hundreds before it pupates. A predator of a different sort is the *aphid wasp*, here shown laying its egg inside an aphid. After hatching, the aphid wasp larva kills and eats its host and pupates in the empty shell. At upper left, a

pair of *blister beetles* searches for the mining bee's burrow; they will parasitize it in much the same way as does the cuckoo bee *(previous page)*. At lower left, a *giant cotton bee* returns to her burrow with a load of pollen that will become the food for her larvae—if they can survive the ravages of the *four-spined cuckoo wasp*. This parasite tunnels down beside the cotton bee's burrow to lay its egg. When the egg hatches, the grub of the wasp finds a ready meal in one of the larvae of the cotton bee. Near

the top of the lupine plant an *adult hover fly*—which, unlike its carnivorous larvae, lives on nectar—is about to be attacked by a *sand wasp*, which will take the victim back to feed its larvae. Another sand wasp has been attacked and killed by a *robber fly* (*bottom, center*). One of the most voracious carnivores of the dunes, this fly paralyzes its prey by stinging it, sucking out all the juices and leaving an empty shell. The red and black *click beetle* clinging to a dead branch (*top right*) is waiting for night,

when it becomes active. The pebble nest below it is the handiwork of the *resin bee*, which glues pebbles with resin garnered from gummy plant secretions to form a receptacle for honey and eggs. At the extreme right is a nest made solely of resin by a close relative, the *little resin bee*. Another night hunter is the huge *katydid wasp*, which preys upon the *wingless katydid*. At lower right, a *cricket wasp* has killed a *field cricket*, which will be added to others stored for its young in the wasp's burrow.

RED VELVET ANT

ASHY GRA
LADYBIRD
BEETLE

ACMON
BLUE BUTTERFLY
(MALE)

THICK-
HEADED FLY

HAIR-STREAK
BUTTERFLY

PEA APHID

ACMON
BLUE BUTTERFLY
(FEMALE)

LADYBIRD BEETLE
LARVA

ACMON BLUE
CATERPILLAR

JUNE BEETLE HUNTER

JUNE BEETLE GRUB

JUNE BEETLE

CLICK BEETLE LARVA

Immune to predators, a big, tough-skinned *red velvet ant*, actually a species of wasp that feeds on sweet plant juices, wings above a lotus plant at upper left. Just below it a *hair-streak butterfly* gathers nectar, while on the ground a *June beetle hunter* locates a *June beetle grub* beneath the surface. The hunter will now dig down and deposit its egg beside the grub, which will later feed the hunter's larva. Nearby, a *June beetle* has pupated and is emerging from the earth as an adult. A *click beetle larva* below it feeds on the roots of the lotus, while aboveground a caterpillar of the *Acmon blue butterfly* eats the stem as male and female adults fly above it, near a *thick-headed fly* sipping nectar. Clustered on another lotus plant, *pea aphids* suck its juices complacently while a *ladybird beetle larva* feeds on one of their number, as does the *ashy gray ladybird beetle* high above. A *brown hoverfly* wings in search of nectar-bearing blossoms, while a *sandhill skipper* lays its eggs below. On a leaf below the sandhill skipper lies a dead *ladybird*

BROWN
HOVER FLY

ANT LION

STINK BUG

SAND WASP

THICK-HEADED FLY

SPINELESS
CUCKOO WASP

SANDHILL SKIPPER

LADYBIRD
BEETLE

COTTON BEE

APHID HUNTER

JERUSALEM CRICKET

MINUTE
CUCKOO WASP

beetle, killed by an aphid wasp larva. A *minute cuckoo wasp*, seeking to lay its egg among aphids in an aphid hunter's burrow, has been attacked by the *aphid hunter* and has rolled itself into a tight ball for defense. The long-winged *adult ant lion* at top, voracious as a larva, has emerged into a less aggressive adulthood; it rests on the grasses by day and flies by night. Here a *stink bug* feeds beside it. A *thick-headed fly* rides on the back of a *sand wasp*, forcing apart its abdominal segments and laying an egg in its body.

Though it survives the larva for a while, the wasp eventually crawls into its burrow and dies while the fly larva pupates within. Lying in a neighboring burrow, a *Jerusalem cricket* waits for night to venture out to forage for food. At lower right, a *cotton bee* inside her burrow fills the top cell with pollen. She has already filled the lower cell, laid an egg and sealed it—but shortly the *spineless cuckoo wasp* just above will dig down and lay an egg that will hatch into a larva that will feed on the larval cotton bee.

3

Northwest from Mexico

"THE Spaniards have notice of seven cities which old men of the Indians show them should lie toward the northwest from Mexico," wrote a 16th Century historian. "They have used and use daily much diligence in seeking of them, but they cannot find any one of them." These were the fabled Seven Cities of Cibola. Reputedly rich in gold and other treasure, they had stirred the imagination of the conquistadors since they first heard of them from exploring parties pushing northward from conquered Mexico. Finally, in 1540, General Francisco Vásquez de Coronado led a full-scale expedition—"the most brilliant company ever collected in the Indies to go in search of new lands"—to locate the seven cities and plunder them. Marching northward from Compostela, on the west coast of Mexico, were 230 caballeros, 62 foot soldiers, friars with their own military escort to convert the heathen, nearly a thousand Indian servants, and 1,500 horses, mules and meat animals. Two years later Coronado returned. Led on by the mirage of a myth, he had trudged through northern Mexico, Arizona, New Mexico, Texas, Oklahoma and Kansas. He had seen more of the vast inland of America than any European—but he was a broken man, his army gone, and without gold, although he had found the seven cities.

Coronado had been swallowed up in an arid expanse left blank by early mapmakers and labeled only as "the great American desert." This huge unexplored area extended from what today is western Texas to the coastal mountain ranges of southern California, and from Oregon southward into Mexico. It is an area of tremendous diversity of landscapes, from valleys below sea level to mountain ranges, all of which have in common heat, dryness and sparsely vegetated land, much of it with bare soil exposed. The deserts of North America have been less disturbed by man than other biomes on the continent, but this does not mean that they have been untouched. To the untrained eye it may seem that they are unchanged, since they have not been flagrantly ravished by ax and plow. But an ecologist notices that the introduction of cattle has drastically altered the distribution and relative abundance of desert plants. Furthermore, mammals and birds have been no more immune to shooting and trapping in the desert than elsewhere, although these direct assaults have been less damaging than the subtler changes man has worked in the environment.

THROUGH countless generations, the animals, plants and Indians of the desert had been able to adjust to its rigors. The invading Spaniards, however, were new to the country and did not know how to adapt to it. As he marched north from Compostela, Coronado found himself penetrating the Sonoran desert, an eroded barrenness where nothing was useful to his forces. Had he delayed his start a few months, he would have found the whole appearance of the desert drastically altered, for after the late spring rains, grasses and numerous kinds of annuals carpet the hard-baked ground, trees break into leaf, and flowering vines climb rapidly up the trunks. But he was there in late winter and saw only rocky, arid plains and range after range of waterless, flinty mountains. By the time the expedition had reached what is now the Arizona-Mexico border, some of his men and animals had already perished; all the others were gaunt, thirsty and on short rations. The desert Indians knew how to get nourishment from the seeds and fruit of desert plants, and even made a preserve from the fruit of the prickly pear cactus. But when the Spaniards tried this, the expedition chronicles record, "the men of the army ate much of it, they all fell sick with a headache and fever."

The Sonoran desert is deceptive. It appears less barren than other North American deserts like the Great Basin, between the Rockies and the Sierra-Cascades, or the Chihuahuan of north-central Mexico and southern New Mexico. It is the richest in cacti, a group of plants native to the New World. Of the 1,600 species of cacti, only five grow outside of the Americas. Moreover, these five, found in Ceylon and South Africa and identical with American species, were not noted until the last century—they were probably introduced accidentally, like Old World plants that now grow as weeds in North America.

Most conspicuous of the Sonoran cacti is the saguaro, the world's largest cactus, its thick columns rising to as high as 40 feet. In the mountain foothills to the west and southeast of Tucson, Arizona, saguaros stretch as far as the eye can see, yet they have been in decline since the end of the last century and today are failing to reproduce themselves. These impressive plants, which normally live to ages of 150 to 200 years, have always had natural hazards to contend with: toppling in high winds or because their roots wash out, freezing in exceptionally cold winters and succumbing to disease. These losses are offset by the enormous numbers of seeds they cast to the winds each June—as many as 400,000 from a single mature plant. Although very few of these seeds ever germinate, enough do—or did, in the past—to ensure the survival of the species. The balance tipped against the saguaros in the 1880s when immense numbers of cattle were introduced into Arizona. Overgrazing radically disturbed the desert's protective plant cover; the result was widespread erosion, intense flooding that uprooted young cacti, lowering of the water table and other marked alterations in the physical environment. Similarly, the recurrent cattleman's war against coyotes led to an increase in the rodent populations, which the coyotes had normally kept down. Desert rodents are extremely destructive of young saguaro plants. When 800 seedlings were set out in an experimental plot, 786 of them were eaten by rats and mice in the first six months, and the remaining 14 plants within two years.

Thus the present failure of the saguaro to reproduce is a part of the larger picture of modern man's incursions on the plant and animal communities of the desert. Attempts are now being made to save the saguaros, but their future in most places is bleak. The greatest stand of saguaros anywhere—in the very area set aside to preserve them evermore, the Saguaro National Monument near Tucson—has deteriorated so far along the path to destruction that they are probably doomed, despite attempts being made to restore the coyote as a rodent controller. And along with the saguaros will also disappear a profusion of birds that have evolved ways of life centered around these desert giants. The huge columns of saguaros are peppered with holes dug into their pulp by Gila woodpeckers and gilded flickers. Since neither bird uses the same hole for more than a single breeding season, the cavity later becomes living quarters for a succession of other birds, such as screech and elf owls, sparrow hawks, purple martins and crested flycatchers.

REDUCTION in the number of predators has been a boon to desert rodents, which already had evolved an array of behavioral and physiological adaptations to the demands placed on them by their environment. Most of these adaptations help the rodents conserve water and avoid heat. The kangaroo rat is able to conserve body water because it possesses an extraordinarily efficient kidney that requires only about a fourth of the water used by the human kidney to excrete the same amount of urea. It avoids the heat by remaining underground during the day, emerging from its burrow only at night, when the air and soil are cool. The trade rat, so called because of its habit of exchanging some object it has been carrying for another, also remains in its humid burrow during the heat of day. In addition, it has a low rate of metabolism, which reduces the amount of energy it expends, and consequently its water loss.

Other kinds of desert rodents are abroad during the day and must endure the same conditions that Coronado's army did. The antelope ground squirrel, which closely resembles a chipmunk, emerges from its burrow at sunrise and must contend with the heat of day. Like most mammals, it uses up large amounts of body water—as much as 10 per cent of its total body weight—in order to keep its temperature down through respiration and evaporation through its skin. Making the problem of water use even more difficult for the antelope ground squirrel is its constant activity. The explanation of its ability to survive the daytime conditions of the desert lies in a cluster of adaptations. Like the kangaroo rat, it possesses an efficient kidney which makes the best possible use of the plants, insects and carrion on which it feeds. But the most important adaptation is its ability to endure a high environmental temperature—the highest for any nonsweating mammal. It can endure a temperature above 100° F. without having to resort to evaporative cooling. It can, in fact, run a fever, allowing its body temperature to rise as the temperature of the environment rises. Actually, it is temporarily storing heat rather than wasting water in an attempt to keep cool. But if its temperature does rise dangerously high, to about 110° F., it can unload the heat it has accumulated simply by returning to the coolness of its burrow and resting until its body temperature has dropped once again.

Coronado's men could not fail to have seen the scampering ground squirrels and the numerous diurnal lizards of the desert, but they apparently paid little attention to either. Lizards are one group that has not been decimated by European man for food, sport or simply to rid the landscape of animals regarded as noxious—the fate of many other North American mammals, birds, fishes and snakes. The rise and fall of lizard populations, up to now, at least, has been determined by environmental factors rather than by man's direct influence. Furthermore, they are alert, quick little animals, and remarkably good at concealing themselves. A number of them take refuge in rock crevices, and the best known of these is the chuckwalla. When pursued, it crawls into a crack and inflates its body with air, wedging itself in so tightly that it cannot be pulled out. Other lizards are burrowers. The horned lizard, or "horned toad," is exceedingly flattened and buries itself by rapid sidewise movements of its body, the edges acting like knives that cut into the desert sand. First one edge of the body tilts downward into the sand, shoving some grains onto its back; then the opposite edge of the body is tilted, throwing up more sand. By such a succession of rapid sidewise movements, the lizard quickly descends belly first.

ONE group of Southwestern sand lizards, members of the genus *Uma*, surpasses all others in the ability to burrow, almost miraculously disappearing into the earth to escape from heat or enemies. The fringe-toed sand lizard is aided by a number of structural adaptations, one of which is the shape of its body. It is somewhat flattened like the horned lizard, but it is also sufficiently elongated to be able to swim through the sands as well as dive in head first. This lizard achieves rapid forward motion with the aid of fringes of scales on its toes that act like paddles. The tip of its snout is sharp, like a wedge, and its nostrils and ear openings are equipped with valves that keep sand out.

More interesting to Coronado's men were the larger animals. "Gray lions and leopards were seen," wrote the chronicler, and he presumably meant the mountain lion and the jaguar. One could hardly fail to overlook the mountain lion—also known as puma, cougar, catamount, panther and painter—and Coronado's observation was but the first of many made by later conquistadors and settlers. Even after centuries of persecution by man, the mountain lion is still probably the most widely distributed mammal in the New World. It ranges from northern British Columbia to Patagonia. In North America it is found throughout much of the western portion of the continent, and there are also some isolated populations in Florida. But it is still probably most abundant in the region in which Coronado sighted it, where it ranges from near sea level in the Arizona desert to the tops of mountains in the southern Rockies of New Mexico and southern Colorado.

No sooner was the desert country opened up by explorers and settlers than a vast body of folklore began to collect around the mountain lion; indeed, few mammals have been the object of greater dread or superstition. A perennial bit of folklore refers to its fierceness, yet there are only a few documented cases of unprovoked attacks on humans, and those may have been by rabid animals. Certainly attacks on humans are contrary to the mountain lion's normal behavior, which is to flee if possible. Even when cornered, it puts up much less of a fight than the smaller bobcat. Nor does the mountain lion emit the blood-curdling screams it is supposed to when advancing on human prey. This is a creature of stealth, and it stalks noiselessly. One category of story told about it, though, is true—the harrowing tales related by pioneers of being tracked for long periods by the big cats. Before the mountain lion had to learn to be wary of humankind, it often followed travelers quite closely, presumably out of mere curiosity. Also correct were early assessments of its power, evidenced by its ability to lug the carcass of an animal several times its own weight over rough terrain and up rocky slopes to its den. Rarely exceeding eight feet in length and 200 pounds in weight, it is nonetheless a formidable animal, with only the bears and the jaguar larger, and none more agile.

Although it also preys on mammals from rodents up to elk, the mountain lion's primary food source is the fleet deer, and there is probably no place on the continent where it thrives in the absence of this prey. In search of deer, the lion seems to follow extensive hunting circuits that may take a week or two to complete. In killing it makes full use of its agility, its weight and its long teeth and claws. Sometimes it stalks in a low crouch, catlike, until it is close enough to spring on the neck of its victim. Sometimes it waits on a ledge over a trail. In either case, the force of its spring and the weight of its body are usually sufficient to bring down its prey. If the deer does not die from a broken neck, it is immediately dispatched by the lion's teeth; the claws are used only for grasping. This hunting procedure is extremely successful. One study indicated that mountain lions manage to kill deer in one out of every three attempts.

The other big cat mentioned by Coronado's expedition, the "leopard," must have been a jaguar. It is the only large-sized spotted feline known in North America, and has a strong superficial resemblance to the leopards of Africa and Asia. This animal, known in Mexico as *el tigre*, is still found in wilder regions there, and once ranged north across the border as far east as Arkansas. Early in the Spanish Colonial administration a bounty was put on its head and its numbers dwindled rapidly. Today it is considered extirpated from the United States, even though individual animals are sometimes found north of Mexico. Jaguars are great wanderers. They follow river valleys and occasionally penetrate deep into the Southwest along the Rio Grande, Pecos, Gila or Colorado.

I T is not surprising that Coronado's party should have singled out for notice the big North American cats, but one wonders why no observations were made of other unusual and abundant species through whose range the army passed. In particular, it is strange that there was no mention of seeing herds of collared peccaries, known also as javelinas. It is possible that the size of his force might have scared them off, for smaller parties of later travelers continuously met these sharp-tusked swinelike beasts. Today about 150,000 of them still live north of Mexico in Arizona, New Mexico and particularly Texas. Although more than 5,000 are shot each year, they have actually increased in the past decade. South of the border, they are even more numerous. Though overhunted in Mexico for food and hides, they have displayed a remarkable ability to persist. In part, this is because they abound wherever there is dense scrubby vegetation, whether mesquite thickets or even cutover forests. They move in small bands of up to 20 individuals. When in danger, the first reaction of the

THE USES OF SCENTS

Both these animals of the Southwest are equipped with musk glands that enable them to secrete pungent odors, but each uses the scent in different ways. The spotted skunk, when threatened, rises on its front feet (above), and if bothered further, lowers its hind feet to the ground, aiming and shooting its noxious fluid, often at the eyes of its enemy. It can hit accurately within a range of 12 feet. The peccary, by contrast, emits its foul scent haphazardly when frightened; more normally, it uses its scent to mark foraging trails, rubbing the opening of the musk gland against bushes and trees (below).

band is to run; peccaries explode in all directions, and anyone in the path of the rushing animals is likely to be slashed by the razor-sharp tusks. However, if there is no dense cover for them to flee into, the band forms a circle, heads facing outward, and stubbornly maintains the ring despite attack. Although coyotes and bobcats sometimes can pick off an unwary animal, their only serious enemy, besides man with his rifle, is the jaguar.

When disturbed, the collared peccary emits a pungent, musky odor, described by an American trapper as "not less offensive than our polecat." The peccary's secretion is produced by a combination of internal oil and sweat from glands which lead to an opening about eight inches above the peccary's tiny tail. This gland opening at first confused the scientists who examined dead specimens brought to Europe. The French taxonomist Baron Cuvier thought that it was a second, misplaced, navel, and he gave the peccary the scientific name *Dicotyles* (derived from two Greek words that mean "two cup-shaped hollows"). The secretion is under the control of the peccary, and when it is annoyed or danger threatens, it is ejected, thus warning the rest of the band, and probably at the same time distracting a predator.

TWO THAT PREVAILED

The natural distribution of most mammals in North America has narrowed before the advance of modern civilization. The nine-banded armadillo and coyote, however, have actually expanded their ranges, as shown on these two pages. The black areas on the maps show present distribution, the color the original range. The armadillo (above) has in fact profited by the reduction of its enemies and wandered from Mexico to east of the Mississippi. Escaped pets launched the Florida colony, which has almost tripled its range in the past 10 years.

ANOTHER animal that Coronado's expedition failed to mention is one of the strangest on the continent, the nine-banded armadillo. Unlike many other mammals and birds that have retreated southward to remote areas of Mexico since the onset of development in the United States desert, the armadillo has actually extended its range northward and eastward. It was not discovered north of the Mexican boundary until 1854, when it was first reported by John James Audubon in southern Texas—and painted by him as somewhat resembling a pig inside a turtle's shell. Since then the animal has steadily extended its range by natural spread, reaching Oklahoma, Kansas, Arkansas, Louisiana and Mississippi, and—with the inadvertent help of man—Alabama and Florida. A few armadillos brought into Florida as pets about the time of World War I, in addition to others which escaped from zoos, have so multiplied that they are now found everywhere in the state save the southern swamps and the northwestern panhandle. The old Aztec word for armadillo means tortoise-rabbit; its modern name comes from the Spanish word *armado*, or "armored." Both are appropriate. With the sole exception of its naked ears, the entire top of the animal from snout to tip of tail is encased in armor. Its body is covered front and back by large bony plates that are joined by nine thin hoops; a flat plate extends over its head from the crown to the end of the nose; the tail is protected by a series of rings, and even the stubby legs are covered by hard scales. But unlike one species of South American armadillo, which can defend itself against predators by rolling itself up into a virtually unassailable ball, the nine-banded armadillo gets only a certain measure of protection from its armor. The scales do serve it much as chaps serve a cowboy: the animal can rush headlong into thorny brush, so tangled that other animals cannot follow. But it is not immune to predation—coyotes, dogs and the larger cats can tear away the armored plates and feed on its tender flesh.

Six months after setting out from Mexico with much pomp and high hopes, Coronado's army was in desperate straits, bedraggled and exhausted, with only two bushels of corn between it and starvation. Not one of the Seven Cities of Cibola had been found, but near what is now Gallup, New Mexico, the soldiers saw on the far horizon a massive four-story structure, its walls gleaming like gold in the sun. They excitedly rushed upon it, only to find that it was an adobe building, a Zuñi Indian pueblo. In fury and despair, they assaulted it, their thirst for treasure at last replaced by a more fundamental need: "There we found something we prized more than gold or silver, namely much maize, beans and chickens larger than those here of New Spain." In the ensuing weeks Coronado located five more Zuñi pueblos; *these* were the golden cities of Cibola. He never found the seventh; it was either legendary or long abandoned. In an empty gesture, he took possession of the six cities for Spain.

Despite the dearth of material riches, Coronado had discovered the most elaborate New World civilization north of Mexico. He was eventually to locate 71 pueblos of an ancient Indian people who had developed irrigation, architecture and crafts to a high degree. Some of these communities were very old. One of them—Pueblo Bonito in northwestern New Mexico—already had about 800 rooms and a population of more than 1,000 people when William the Conqueror invaded England; it remained North America's most spacious apartment house until 1882. But Coronado was not interested in ancient civilizations. Disheartened, he sent out reconnaissance parties to learn if riches lay still farther afield. One of his groups rode northwestward and discovered atop three mesas, or flattop mountains, in Arizona a cluster of Hopi villages. It was also reported that the countryside abounded with "humpback cows"—the American bison, which before the coming of European man, ranged from northern Canada to northeastern Mexico. Another band marched eastward and reached the numerous pueblos of the upper Rio Grande in the vicinity of what is now Santa Fe; but like the Zuñi pueblos, these also lacked gold or silver.

A third column—about a dozen men under Don García López de Cárdenas traveled to the northwest and made the most spectacular discovery of all, the Grand Canyon of the Colorado River. Cárdenas was the first European to experience what is undoubtedly the greatest visual shock on the continent. But he was not as enraptured as the multitudes of visitors who travel to Grand Canyon today; to him, the abyss merely meant an obstacle he must surmount "which seemed to be more than three or four leagues in an air line across to the other bank of the stream." The old Spanish league was about two and a half miles, and thus Cárdenas' estimate was between seven and 10 miles; actually the distance from rim to rim varies between four and 18 miles.

C ARDENAS did not long pause to admire the brilliant colors of the chasm; he had journeyed across northern Arizona in the blistering heat of midsummer and his water supply was low. Now he was in sight of abundant water, but it flowed far below his reach—"which looked from above as if the water was six feet across, although the Indians said it was half a league wide." For three days Cárdenas attempted to find a way to descend to the Colorado River; some of his men managed to get about a third of the way down but could go no farther. However, they did confirm that the river appeared to be large indeed, and decided that the width given by the Indians was correct. This was but the first of many exaggerations that would be made about the Grand Canyon; instead of being half a league across, the Colorado River at that point has a width of only about 100 yards. Cárdenas and his men turned back, leaving the Grand Canyon to be unseen by a European for another two centuries, when a lone Spanish missionary would coax his mule down a narrow ledge. "They cause horror, these precipices," the missionary recorded. Unbelievingly, as if he had descended to the depths of hell itself, he found human life at the bottom. There on the floor of the canyon, cultivating about 400 acres of flat land—as they

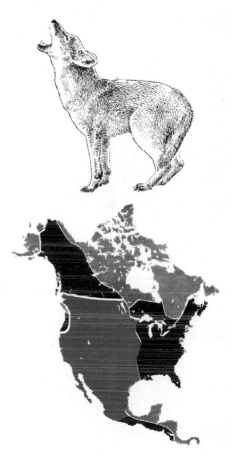

One of the most persistent and adaptable of all North American mammals, the coyote originally lived in the western plains and the rugged uplands of northern Mexico. But in the last 400 years, lured by European man's livestock and harried by his persecution, the coyote has extended its range enormously. Following the Spaniards, it penetrated southern Mexico in the 16th Century, and in the 19th had worked its way north into British Columbia. By the turn of the century, it had reached Alaska. Meanwhile it was also spreading eastward and has now been reported everywhere in New England and New York State except for Long Island and New York City itself.

still do today—was an Indian tribe, the Havasupai, one of the most isolated people on earth. Neither the Havasupai nor the precarious descent are quite so startling as the fact that the missionary failed to record one word about the overwhelming grandeur of the canyon. For the explorers, the canyon was merely there; it brought forth no hyperbole about its beauty, only dismay at their inability to cross it. Later on, settlers were similarly blind to the beauties of the canyonland country. Ebenezer Bryce once described the magnificent canyon in Utah that today bears his name as "a hell of a place to lose a cow."

The 220-mile-long gash that the Grand Canyon makes in the earth's surface is the result of a combination of ingredients and events so unusual that the probability of its occurring again is remote indeed. First, there had to be easily eroded rock, miles deep. The Colorado Plateau—a vast tableland that covers nearly 130,000 square miles in northern Arizona, northern New Mexico, western Colorado and southern Utah—provided that. It is composed of layer atop layer of soft sedimentary rock, laid down during hundreds of millions of years when this area was periodically flooded by seas. Second, these deep strata had to be uplifted by shifts in the earth's crust to form dry land. Third, there had to be a river running across the plateau, not only a powerful river but also a swift-running one so that the large amounts of sediment it carried could act as an abrasive to cut into its rockbed. The Colorado River fulfilled this requirement. The second longest river in the United States, it flows at speeds of up to 20 miles an hour and, on the average, carries half a million tons of abrasive sand and silt through the Grand Canyon every day. Finally, although it was necessary for the plateau to rise, its uplift could not be faster than the cutting action of the river, or else it would have spilled the Colorado out of its course. All these factors worked together. As the Colorado Plateau rose at the beginning of the Tertiary (a great mountain-building period that saw the rise of the Rockies and Pacific Coast ranges also), the river scoured out its bed at approximately the same speed as the uplift occurred. The process was much the same as if one held a rotary saw steady and slowly raised a block of wood upward against the blade.

Coronado's route across southern Arizona had taken him through possibly the richest center of bird life on the continent, almost a fourth of the approximately 800 species of birds of North America nest in the southeastern quarter of Arizona. His men undoubtedly had a chance to observe some of the more unusual species. They could scarcely have missed the odd-looking, long-legged bird of prey, Audubon's caracara, sitting as still as a stuffed bird atop a tall cactus as it watched for prey. Also, they must have noted the comical roadrunner, which sprints across the desert in search of lizards and snakes, insects and rodents, chasing almost anything that moves. Today rarely seen outside of the undeveloped parts of the desert, the roadrunner once ranged the arid plains and hills from Kansas to the Pacific Ocean and southward into the northern half of Mexico. This bird is so determinedly pedestrian that the belief has grown that it cannot fly. This is not true; not only does it make long glides from hillsides to valleys but it can also fly about an eighth of a mile under its own power. It does, though, rely mostly on its legs for locomotion, aided by a fluttering of its stubby wings for extra speed, much in the manner of an ostrich. Other birds that Coronado might have seen were three species of strangely decorated quail—Gambel's quail with a showy plume atop its head, the masked bobwhite with its brilliant colors, the harlequin or "fool quail"

THE NIMBLE ROADRUNNER

A foot-long tail, powerful legs, and feet with claws which grip the ground X-fashion, two pointing forward, two behind, make the desert roadrunner one of the most nimble of all animals on the ground. It has been clocked at 15 miles an hour at full speed (top picture), head outthrust, tail streaming behind; yet in an instant it can swerve into a turn (center pictures), using its tail as a brake or rudder. For a fast stop (bottom picture) the tail is spread wide and thrust up and forward, sometimes right over the bird's head. So quick is this bird that it can and does outstrike a rattlesnake and is capable of killing it with its sharp beak.

which was so trusting of humankind. Gambel's quail is still fairly abundant in the Southwest, the once-fearless harlequin quail is now a vanishing species and the masked bobwhite is virtually extinct. The last masked bobwhite known to have been shot in the United States was killed in 1885, but scattered survivors probably managed to linger in southern Arizona until the beginning of this century. Now they have become rare in the Sonoran desert of Mexico also; a dozen years ago, a very diligent ornithological search there turned up only a few birds. The explanation for their decline is destruction of their habitat by introduced cattle, a plight worsened by drought.

THE chronicle of the Coronado expedition did mention a few birds seen in the pueblos: "In this country there were also tame eagles, which the chiefs esteemed. . . . There are a great many native fowl . . . and cocks with great hanging chins." The cocks with the hanging chins were probably the descendants of Merriam's turkeys, a hardy mountain-dwelling race once found in the Southwest, and domesticated by the Pueblo Indians long before the arrival of Coronado. Merriam's turkey is adjusted to life in a very distinctive habitat: the ponderosa pine-oak forests that grow between 6,000 and about 10,000 feet from central Colorado nearly to the Mexican border. A mature Merriam's gobbler in mating display is assuredly a magnificent sight, and "great hanging chins" is a gross understatement. The embellishments on the bird's head may dangle in velvet-textured folds for nearly a foot, their colors varying from flamingo red to azure blue. The back, neck and breast feathers are black, but have a bronze sheen when the sun strikes them. Even in primeval times the wild population of Merriam's turkey was probably never very large, perhaps no more than a quarter of a million birds in the three states of Colorado, Arizona and New Mexico. Like much of the bird life of the continent, it has suffered since the arrival of man. A survey in 1942 estimated its total population at about 40,000; conservation efforts since then have probably increased this figure somewhat.

Both golden and bald eagles once nested almost throughout the continent, but nowadays the chances of seeing an eagle soaring in the wild are rare, for both birds have become alarmingly scarce. A search by hundreds of professional and amateur ornithologists a few years ago to locate all the bald eagles in the United States exclusive of Alaska turned up only seven in Arizona and 21 in New Mexico. In fact, only 3,807 bald eagles were found, and half of their nests were in Florida. Although this bird is the national emblem of the United States, it was not protected against shooting until 1940. This tardy step has not arrested the precipitous decline. Shooting was originally the prime cause of the dwindling numbers, but today the eagles must also contend with the encroachment of civilization, loss of nesting trees as a result of logging and storms, and possibly indirect poisoning by feeding on animals that have concentrated large amounts of insecticide in their body fat.

Everywhere that Coronado went in the Pueblo Indian country he found an abundance of corn, or maize. Explorers who came after him from Mexico could not believe that the Indians' cultivation of maize in irrigated fields was a native art; they commented on the "many irrigated maize fields with canals and dams as if Spaniards had built them." Nevertheless, irrigation and cultivation of corn were ancient arts in the Southwest. Abandoned pueblos along the Salt River of Arizona reveal that a quarter of a million acres must have been under irrigation in that valley alone; remnants of the irrigation works at Mesa Verde, Colorado, show that the ancestors of the modern Pueblo Indians had mastered the technology just as well as the peoples who developed the high civilizations of the eastern Mediterranean.

Corn was the New World's most important food plant. It was grown from the St. Lawrence valley southward to central Chile, and formed the basis for such elaborate cultures of pre-Columbian America as the Aztec and Pueblo communities. There is not a single bit of evidence that it ever grew outside of the New World before 1492. So ancient a crop was it that when early explorers found it being cultivated by Indians all over North America, it already existed in most of the varieties known today. There have been two major mysteries about corn: how long ago, and where, was it first domesticated? Until recently, the only answers that could be given were vague: "many thousands" of years ago, "probably" in Mexico or in Peru. But in 1960, several caves once inhabited by prehistoric man were discovered about 150 miles south of Mexico City, in the Tehuacan Valley, and a total of 23,607 specimens of maize were uncovered by archeologists digging in the refuse of their floors. These layers of refuse read like the pages of a book, with the bottommost layer being the most ancient and thus providing the first chapter. At that bottom level, dated at least 7,200 years ago, cobs of wild corn were found, miniature affairs compared to today's large ears. It was a rather unpromising plant on which to erect the great civilizations of ancient America, probably little more conspicuous than some of the wild grasses that grow as weeds in gardens today. Then, some time between 7,200 and 5,400 years ago, the cave excavations reveal a change in the corn ears; they grew larger, probably an indication that man was weeding, thus encouraging their growth by removing competition from other plants, and probably also making a start in irrigation. Between 5,400 and 4,300 years ago, there can be no doubt that full-scale agriculture was underway—for a hybrid maize was being grown, in addition to other crop plants such as gourds, beans, chili peppers and avocados. Finally, maize found in the upper layers of these caves reveals a distinct evolutionary sequence of cultivated varieties—including several kinds still being grown in Mexico today.

Was this the start of domestic corn? Possibly not in those exact caves or at that exact time. But this evidence strongly suggests the Mexican plateau as having been the place, and seven thousand years ago as the approximate date. It is interesting that man's other great agricultural innovation, the domestication of wheat, is believed to have taken place in the Near East not very much earlier —about 8,500 years ago.

T HERE can be no underestimating the importance of corn to the New World Indians as it spread north and south from Mexico. No doubt it reached the ancestors of today's Pueblo Indians very early, but it was probably not until nearly 2,000 years ago that different varieties were diffused widely in the prairies and eastern Indian cultures. Coronado had no appreciation of the value of this new crop, or of the land itself. Since he had found no gold, he regarded himself as a failure—as did his contemporaries. A few, among them Pedro de Castañeda, the chronicler of the ill-fated expedition, felt differently. He realized the wealth of another kind that this land might produce, and he wrote of his comrades on the expedition: "Granted that they did not find the riches of which they had been told, they found a place in which to search for them, and the beginning of a good country to settle in. . . . Their hearts weep for having lost so favorable an opportunity."

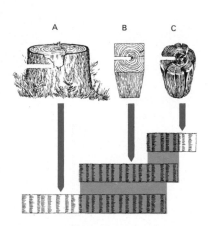

THE RINGS OF TIME

Calculating the age of wood by studying its rings enables archeologists to establish dates of ancient pueblos and also to read the climatic story of the Southwest. In a given area, the pattern of rings for all the trees growing at the same time is essentially the same, since ring size depends on weather—a narrow ring means a dry year, a wide ring a wet one. Therefore, by matching the overlapping patterns of the rings of hundreds of samples going back through time, a historical chronology may be established. In a recently cut tree (A, above), its oldest inner rings match the pattern in the outer rings of a beam taken from an old Spanish mission (B), and a step back in time can be taken. The inner rings of the beam, in turn, match the outer rings of a still older wood sample from a pre-Columbian pueblo (C). In this fashion, overlapping ring patterns have been matched all the way back to an Indian pueblo in the Southwest which could now be accurately dated at 59 B.C.

CALLED GUARDIANS, THESE CAREFULLY TENDED ADOBE FIGURES OF UNKNOWN AGE ENCLOSE THE INDIAN CEMETERY AT ACOMA, NEW MEXICO

The Natural People

As much a part of North America as any of its native plants and animals are the Indians, who learned to live not only from the land but with it. Civilization destroyed this natural way of things, and today, their numbers diminished, their cultures compromised, they exist precariously. But in the Southwest, life goes on for some of them much as it once did, amid the monuments of the past.

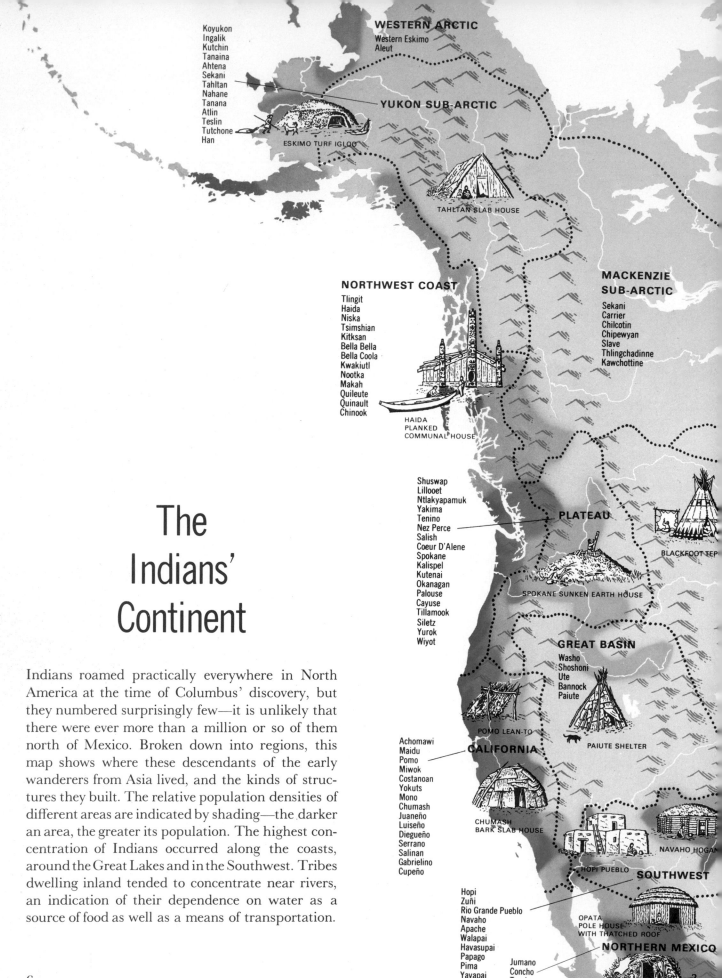

Koyukon
Ingalik
Kutchin
Tanaina
Ahtena
Sekani
Tahltan
Nahane
Tanana
Atlin
Teslin
Tutchone
Han

WESTERN ARCTIC

Western Eskimo
Aleut

ESKIMO TURF IGLOO

YUKON SUB-ARCTIC

TAHLTAN SLAB HOUSE

**MACKENZIE
SUB-ARCTIC**

Sekani
Carrier
Chilcotin
Chipewyan
Slave
Thlingchadinne
Kawchottine

NORTHWEST COAST

Tlingit
Haida
Niska
Tsimshian
Kitksan
Bella Bella
Bella Coola
Kwakiutl
Nootka
Makah
Quileute
Quinault
Chinook

HAIDA
PLANKED
COMMUNAL HOUSE

Shuswap
Lillooet
Ntlakyapamuk
Yakima
Tenino
Nez Perce
Salish
Coeur D'Alene
Spokane
Kalispel
Kutenai
Okanagan
Palouse
Cayuse
Tillamook
Siletz
Yurok
Wiyot

PLATEAU

BLACKFOOT TEP

SPOKANE SUNKEN EARTH HOUSE

GREAT BASIN

Washo
Shoshoni
Ute
Bannock
Paiute

The Indians' Continent

Indians roamed practically everywhere in North America at the time of Columbus' discovery, but they numbered surprisingly few—it is unlikely that there were ever more than a million or so of them north of Mexico. Broken down into regions, this map shows where these descendants of the early wanderers from Asia lived, and the kinds of structures they built. The relative population densities of different areas are indicated by shading—the darker an area, the greater its population. The highest concentration of Indians occurred along the coasts, around the Great Lakes and in the Southwest. Tribes dwelling inland tended to concentrate near rivers, an indication of their dependence on water as a source of food as well as a means of transportation.

Achomawi
Maidu
Pomo
Miwok
Costanoan
Yokuts
Mono
Chumash
Juaneño
Luiseño
Diegueño
Serrano
Salinan
Gabrielino
Cupeño

CALIFORNIA

POMO LEAN-TO

PAIUTE SHELTER

CHUMASH
BARK SLAB HOUSE

NAVAHO HOGAN

HOPI PUEBLO

SOUTHWEST

Hopi
Zuñi
Rio Grande Pueblo
Navaho
Apache
Walapai
Havasupai
Papago
Pima
Yavapai

OPATA
POLE HOUSE
WITH THATCHED ROOF

NORTHERN MEXICO

Jumano
Concho
Tarahumare
Seri
Opatá
Cáhita

SERI BRUSH SHELTER

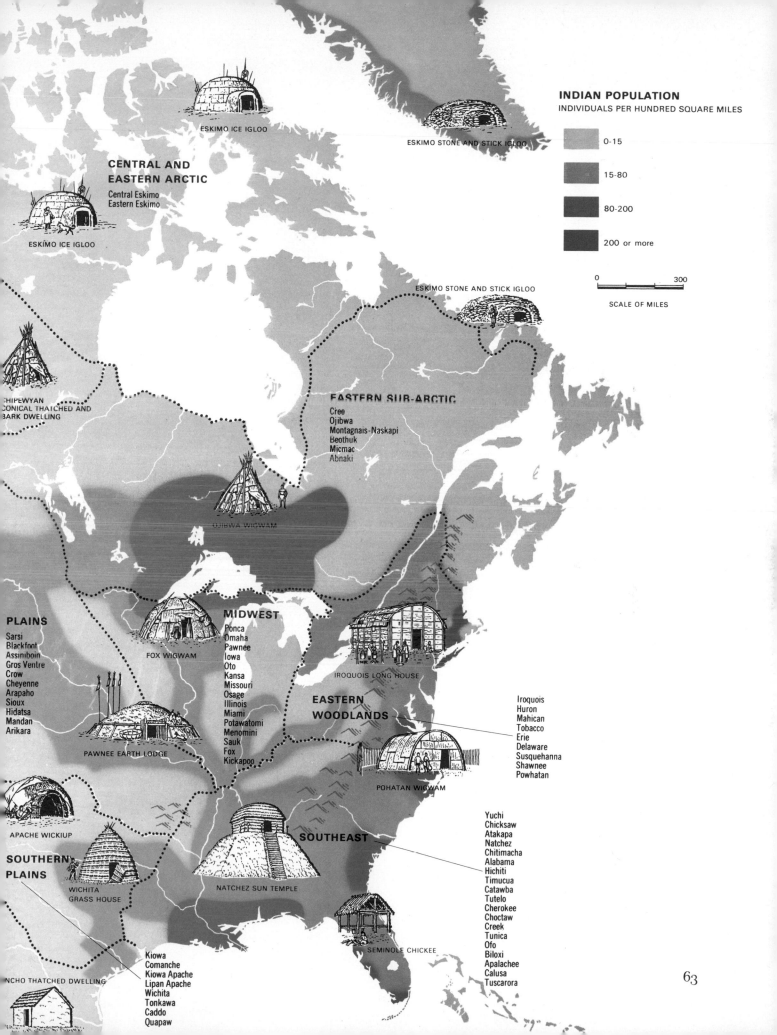

INDIAN POPULATION
INDIVIDUALS PER HUNDRED SQUARE MILES

0-15
15-80
80-200
200 or more

0   300
SCALE OF MILES

ESKIMO ICE IGLOO

ESKIMO STONE AND STICK IGLOO

CENTRAL AND EASTERN ARCTIC

Central Eskimo
Eastern Eskimo

ESKIMO ICE IGLOO

ESKIMO STONE AND STICK IGLOO

CHIPEWYAN
CONICAL THATCHED AND
BARK DWELLING

EASTERN SUB-ARCTIC

Cree
Ojibwa
Montagnais-Naskapi
Beothuk
Micmac
Abnaki

OJIBWA WIGWAM

PLAINS

Sarsi
Blackfoot
Assiniboin
Gros Ventre
Crow
Cheyenne
Arapaho
Sioux
Hidatsa
Mandan
Arikara

FOX WIGWAM

MIDWEST

Ponca
Omaha
Pawnee
Iowa
Oto
Kansa
Missouri
Osage
Illinois
Miami
Potawatomi
Menomini
Sauk
Fox
Kickapoo

IROQUOIS LONG HOUSE

EASTERN WOODLANDS

Iroquois
Huron
Mahican
Tobacco
Erie
Delaware
Susquehanna
Shawnee
Powhatan

PAWNEE EARTH LODGE

POHATAN WIGWAM

APACHE WICKIUP

SOUTHERN PLAINS

WICHITA GRASS HOUSE

SOUTHEAST

NATCHEZ SUN TEMPLE

Yuchi
Chicksaw
Atakapa
Natchez
Chitimacha
Alabama
Hichiti
Timucua
Catawba
Tutelo
Cherokee
Choctaw
Creek
Tunica
Ofo
Biloxi
Apalachee
Calusa
Tuscarora

SEMINOLE CHICKEE

Kiowa
Comanche
Kiowa Apache
Lipan Apache
Wichita
Tonkawa
Caddo
Quapaw

CADDO THATCHED DWELLING

63

WALPI PUEBLO IN NORTHERN ARIZONA DATES BACK TO THE 17TH CENTURY WHEN HOPI INDIANS, IN AN ATTEMPT TO ESCAPE SPANISH PERSECUTION,

The Venerable Ones

Among the Indian tribes still living on lands where white men first saw them, and still pursuing old ways, are the Pueblos and Navahos of the Southwest. The Navahos, along with their blood brothers the Apaches, outnumber the Pueblos today—but they are relative newcomers, having migrated to the region from northwestern Canada perhaps as late as the 14th Century. The Pueblos, on the other hand, can trace their lineage to a people known as the Basket Makers, who settled here at the beginning of the Christian era. Living first in pit homes and then in dwellings above ground, they took to

64

MOVED THEIR VILLAGE TO THE TOP OF THIS MESA FROM A SITE AT ITS BASE. HOPI DERIVES FROM THE WORD "HOPITU," FOR "PEACEFUL ONES"

building joined houses, or pueblos, of two, three or more stories. Some, like the Mesa Verdeans, came to sequester their houses in caves; others erected massive structures out in the open. Pueblo Bonito encompassed over three acres, had up to five stories and approximately 800 rooms for more than 1,000 people. When a disaster—perhaps drought, coupled with soil depletion—blighted this and other pueblos late in the 13th Century, the hard-struck inhabitants scattered south and east. Today, their descendants occupy 27 "new" pueblos, of which 300-year-old Walpi (above) is one of the best known.

MELONS IN A TREE signal the traditional ways of the Pueblos, who still dehydrate many of their foods in the old manner. Here, a Santo Domingo Indian, dressed much like his forebears, hangs up a peeled, hollowed-out melon which, drying slowly in the sun, will shrivel like the fruit on the lower branches, to be stored in a cool place for later use in sauces and pies.

POTTERY ON THE GROUND recalls the artistry of Southwest tribes. Shown clockwise are an ancient Mimbres bowl (*lower left*); a Tewa polychrome jar; an Acoma bowl; a small modern pot; a flared-rim jar and a large jar from Santa Clara; a large Zuñi pot (*top*); a Zia water jar; a Santo Domingo bowl; a Zuñi jar; an old Socorro jar; a modern Hopi bowl.

The Past Preserved

Perched high on its eroded sandstone cliffs, the mesa-top pueblo of Acoma (*opposite*) seems more like a fortress than a town—and in a sense, that is just what it is. Remote from the modern world, it has resisted change, and it provides a picture of what life was like for pueblo dwellers centuries ago. Here are the terraced houses of mud and stone, with their ceremonial kivas and their tiny, smoke-stained rooms, the upper stories still often reached from the outside by ladders and entered through holes in the roof. Here, too, are the granaries, with their stores of corn and wheat, and the grinding bins, where kneeling women still crush dried corn with handstones on sloping metates.

When the Spaniards came north in the late 16th Century to colonize the territory of the Pueblos, they met their first serious resistance here at Acoma. But they scaled the cliffs and took the town, and among the punishments they meted out to the inhabitants was one so cruel it may well have helped make the pueblo the closed community Acoma is even today —all captive males over 25 had one foot cut off.

A CEREMONIAL LADDER, with three poles rather than two, figures in Acoma religious activities. Ladders like these lead to kivas, where such tribal rites as rain making still take place.

THE SPANISH INFLUENCE shows up in outdoor ovens like this one, which bake crusty loaves. Among the few concessions made to an invading culture, this type of baking has still not entirely supplanted the traditional method—corn batter spread on hot stone griddles and peeled off, minutes later, in paper-thin sheets.

PRE-COLUMBIAN ACOMA is one of the oldest continuously inhabited towns in the U.S. Its church (*upper left*) was built by the Spaniards with forced Indian labor. Walls 10 feet thick support beams 40 feet long which the Indians carried across 20 miles of desert and hoisted up the 357-foot-high cliffs.

LIVING IN HOGANS AND HUTS ON LAND AS BARREN AS THIS STRETCH OF ARIZONA DESERT, THE NAVAHOS HAVE MANAGED TO MULTIPLY SINCE

NAVAHO JEWELRY displayed on sand includes objects of turquoise and silver, as well as a prehistoric shell necklace.

The Adaptable Navahos

For the Navahos, survival and success have depended less on the perpetuation of old ways than on the adoption—and transmutation—of new ones. Entering Pueblo territory from the north, they so harassed the local tribes that their victims sought to appease them by teaching them how to plant and raise corn. This gave the seminomadic Navahos a measure of security and enabled them to settle down. They went on to learn weaving from the Pueblos and traders, and sheepherding and horsemanship from the Spaniards. In fact, there is hardly an art or ceremony that the Navahos did not get from someone else. They picked up silverworking from the Mexicans as late as the middle of the 19th Century, taking over not only their methods and tools but many of their designs. Even an art as indelibly Navaho as sand painting (*opposite*) seems to have been learned, as was so much else, originally from the Pueblos.

SETTLING DOWN ON THEIR 25,000-SQUARE-MILE RESERVATION. TODAY THE LARGEST INDIAN TRIBE IN THE U.S., THEY NUMBER MORE THAN 90,000

SPRINKLING DRY PIGMENTS on the ground, a Navaho begins a sand painting. When finished, it will serve a religious-medi- cal purpose—a medicine man will seat his patient on it facing east, then will chant over him and drive away the bad spirits.

The Vanquished

To the north and east of the territories occupied by the Navahos and the Pueblos stretched the grasslands of the plains and midwest Indians—the Dakota Sioux, the Mandan, Iowa, Kansa, Osage, Crow and others. Into this wilderness in the 1830s went George Catlin, a lawyer turned artist, who recorded the life of these tribes at a time when white settlers were yet a rarity in the West. But though the tribes still ruled the grasslands, already there were signs of deterioration. Enticed by the goods of civilization, the tribes had begun the slaughter of the buffalo. Catlin once saw Indians bring in 1,400 buffalo tongues, which they had harvested in one afternoon and for which they were paid a few gallons of cheap whiskey by white traders. "It is not enough," wrote an outraged Catlin, "that we get from the Indian his lands, and the very clothes from his back, but the food for his mouth . . ."

Among the most famous of Catlin's works are his portraits of Indian chiefs (*opposite*). "An Indian," observed an amused Catlin, "often lies down from morning till night in front of his portrait, admiring his beautiful face, and faithfully guarding it from day to day to protect it from accident or harm."

A SCALP DANCE, PAINTED BY CATLIN, BRINGS SIOUX WARRIORS TO A FRENZY AS YOUNG GIRLS IN THE CENTER HOLD UP THE GORY TROPHIES

WILLING SUBJECTS, chiefs from Canada to the southern plains, sat for Catlin. So alert-looking was his portrait of One Horn (*bottom row, center*) that the medicine men worried it couldn't sleep at night.

MAN OF GOOD SENSE

BIG EAGLE

THE OTTAWAY

STURGEONS HEAD

HE WHO HAS EYES BEHIND HIM

WOLF

LITTLE WHITE BEAR

ONE HORN

BLOODY HAND

4

The Southern Lowlands

ONE very good explanation for the faith Coronado and his men held in the existence of the Seven Cities of Cibola was the fantastic hauls made by other conquistadors in other rumored treasure cities. Cortez in Mexico City and Pizarro in Peru with only small armies had overwhelmed two extremely elaborate and sophisticated cultures, and the gold they wrenched from the Indians literally ran to the roomful. Propelled by these rich visions, every Spanish adventurer in the New World had hopes of leading or joining an expedition. Not the least of these was the governor of Cuba, Hernando de Soto, who decided that he would find the Seven Cities himself.

De Soto had no idea where they were, nor of the land and people he would encounter. Nevertheless, he organized an army and in May 1539 he landed near what is now Fort Myers on the west coast of Florida, determined to work his way into the interior of the unknown continent, confident that he would pick up information from Indians as he went along. Ironically, he set out at about the same time that Coronado did. His route was north and then west through the southern lowlands; Coronado's was north from Mexico and then east. At one point elements of his force came within a scant few hundred miles of crossing

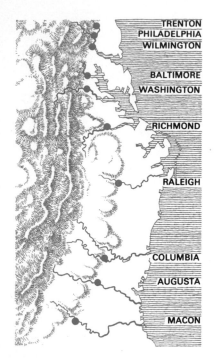

TRENTON
PHILADELPHIA
WILMINGTON

BALTIMORE
WASHINGTON

RICHMOND

RALEIGH

COLUMBIA

AUGUSTA

MACON

CITIES AND WHITE WATER

Many of the major cities of the East (above) have been settled along the fall line, the boundary where rivers and streams plunge from the resistant granite rocks of the Appalachian Mountains to the soft rocks of the coastal plain, thus forming rapids and waterfalls. At first established as trading centers by the pioneers because the falls made further western navigation of the rivers difficult, the towns subsequently blossomed. In the industrial age, the waterfalls became an inexpensive and reliable source of power. The result is a string of important cities from Trenton in the north to Macon in the south, all with white water upstream.

Coronado's path near the Red River in Texas. The environments through which the two conquistadors traveled are in stark contrast. The southwest is barren and arid, the southeast is lush and soggy, and de Soto soon found himself floundering in mile after mile of swamp. Whereas Coronado had little difficulty in subduing the Pueblo Indians, the southeastern tribes (particularly the Creeks, Chickasaws, Choctaws and Cherokees) were extremely warlike. They gave de Soto an unwelcome reception, skirmishing at night, ambushing his men from the shelter of tall canebrakes and from behind thick tree trunks.

THE lowlands encompass a sweeping arc of southeastern United States from Chesapeake Bay southward along the Atlantic and Gulf coastal plains to the Mississippi River. The interior boundary of this arc is sharply delineated by what is known as the "fall line." If all the waterfalls of the coastal plain—the Great Falls of the Potomac above Washington, the falls of the James River at Richmond, the falls of the Chattahoochee River at Columbus, Georgia, and others—are joined by a line on a map, this line will mark the interior boundary of the coastal plain. The explanation for the occurrence of the waterfalls along this line is that here the rivers leave the resistant granitic rocks of the Appalachian foothills and cut downward into the yielding sedimentary rocks of the coastal plain. Today the fall line is marked in another way: many of the major cities of the southeastern states lie just downstream from it. That is because for the pioneers the falls marked the end of river transportation inland; they abandoned their boats there and set up trading centers which eventually grew into major cities.

The landscape of the southern lowlands that greeted de Soto was once composed of a remarkable diversity of scenes—extensive forests of pine, dark cypress swamps and prairies of soggy grass from which rose hummocks of trees like islands. But these habitats have been so intensively logged, burned, drained and farmed that today much of the southern lowlands has a bleak sameness. One must travel far and look hard to find the landscapes that de Soto saw—to the Everglades National Park for sawgrass and hummocks, to Okefenokee National Wildlife Refuge in southern Georgia to see ancient cypresses, to the inaccessible Louisiana bayous to find brooding swamps. Even the meanderings of the lower Mississippi River are now being tamed within the walls of high levees. And many of the animals that de Soto must have seen have vanished utterly or are rare sights indeed. The alligator, once abundant throughout all the southern rivers and swamps, now thrives mainly in southern Florida and in Okefenokee. No more than a handful of Everglades kites still survives, the great ivory-billed woodpecker may be extinct, not a single whooping crane flies through the air of the southeastern lowlands, the Carolina parakeet and passenger pigeon are both gone forever.

De Soto marched northward from western Florida in the hope of soon finding gold, but instead he found only impoverished Indian villages, among them one known as Apalache. It later appeared on Spanish maps to designate the hilly interior; finally, its name changed to Appalachian, it came to refer to the mountains themselves. Much of de Soto's route northward lay across a land covered with virgin pines which the men much admired—"well proportioned and as tall as the tallest in Spain." For weeks he forced his way through a nearly impenetrable barrier of longleaf pines, once one of the most extensive stands of a single tree species in the world, stretching a distance of about 1,500 miles along the coastal plain from Virginia to eastern Texas. This is the tree that rivaled the white pine of the northern states, that grew true as a mast to a height of nearly 100 feet and later led the British Crown to set aside the best stands for the exclusive use of its navy. One can scarcely mistake this tree for any other. For the first six or seven years of the seedling's life, the stem scarcely grows at all, and consequently the dense cluster of needles resembles a thick tuft of grass. But during this "grass stage," as it is called, a tremendous root system is developing underground; once this has become established, the aboveground portion of the tree begins to grow. The bright-green needles of a mature tree reach a length of a foot and a half, making this one of the most graceful of all the pines.

One can still find remnants of this great pine forest, interrupted along streams by stands of live oak and other southern hardwoods. The live oak is a most unoaklike oak. It is distinctive in shape—often twice as wide as it is high. Its leaves—only a few inches long, oval and leathery—also are unlike those of most of the familiar northern oaks, and they stay green throughout the year. The tree was a valuable one for shipbuilding and it was the first species whose cutting was regulated by the United States Government. In 1799, about 350 acres of live-oak forest were set aside for shipbuilding use; by 1845, a quarter of a million acres had been preserved. We would have incomparable live-oak forests today if this acreage still existed, but with the decline in the use of wood for shipbuilding, it was given over to settlers. However, some of the ancient oaks still found in the southern lowlands owe their existence to this early attempt at controlled logging.

Almost everywhere that live oaks grow, one is apt to find them festooned with immense draperies of Spanish moss. This is not a Spanish import to the New World—it was growing in the lowlands long before the arrival of de Soto—nor is it a moss. Rather, it is a member of the pineapple family and it bears a scientific name that is the result of another misconception. The 18th Century Swedish taxonomist Linnaeus knew that these plants led an aerial existence and lacked a root connection with the soil; he concluded that they must abhor water. So he named the plant *Tillandsia* after his friend, the naturalist E. E. Tillandz, who was so prone to seasickness that he once walked 1,000 miles around the Gulf of Bothnia rather than cross it in a boat. Actually, water is a necessity to Spanish moss, despite its desiccated appearance. It grows only in areas of high humidity, where water can be obtained directly from the air, and thus its banners are particularly thick in the river valleys and lowland swamps. Its grayish outer covering is deceptive also, for if one parts the shreds, green chlorophyll cells can be seen—evidence that this is not a parasite upon the live oaks but an honest laborer in the sun, manufacturing its own food by the process of photosynthesis. It uses the tree only as a scaffolding on which it can grow high in the air and catch the sunlight.

Not knowing what to expect in his explorations, de Soto brought with him 13 hogs which he planned to breed during his march as a source of food. By the following spring, their numbers had increased to 300. The huge wild boars found today in the Great Smoky Mountains of North Carolina are sometimes claimed to be descendants of de Soto's hogs, but that is not so; they were imported from Europe in 1912 by British sportsmen. On the other hand, it is quite likely that the somewhat smaller but almost equally vicious wild hogs of the vast Okefenokee swamp are descendants of swine that escaped from de Soto's herds. The hogs were a food supply to be held in reserve, and while the herd was being built up the Spaniards had to live off the land, obtaining

FAREWELL TO A GIANT

In the days of its glory, the American chestnut (above) grew across much of the eastern United States, often rising 100 feet tall. Its nuts, sweet and nourishing, were an essential wildlife food. Today, because of the Asian fungus that has blighted this tree for 60 years, the chestnut exists only in saplings (below), which may sprout from old roots and survive until they reach a height of 25 feet or so. But each year the sprouts grow fewer and the American chestnut will soon disappear forever. Crossbreeding experiments have created some fungus-resistant hybrids, but attempting to replenish the former chestnut forests with these hybrids would be a task for Paul Bunyan.

corn from the Indians when they could. They sampled many strange plants, occasionally finding one like the chestnut, which they described as being "rich and of very good flavor." Other explorers and settlers in the eastern United States, from Maine to southern Alabama, subsequently noted the sweetness of the fruit of the American chestnut, but no one will ever sample it again. This tree has been the victim of an incomparable disaster, the worst suffered by any tree on the continent since the arrival of European man. The disaster was much more subtle than destruction by axes or the blaze of forest fires. It was the result of a fungus blight accidentally carried into North America from Asia. It was first discovered in New York City in 1904, but nothing could be done to halt it and it spread rapidly. Today all that remains of one of the noblest trees on the continent are bleached trunks, naked of leaves. Despite the persistent growth of shoots from old roots, these eventually also succumb to the blight.

In his fruitless search for treasure, de Soto traveled north through Georgia and South Carolina. So far he had found only fresh-water pearls, some of them extremely beautiful and valuable, but these were all stolen again by the Indians in a raid. Still goldless, de Soto turned west and made his way into central Alabama. Here the Indians had already begun the destruction of the southern forest that was to accelerate with the settlements of European man. They had extensive fields of corn and beans, and numerous orchards—"the country, thickly settled in numerous and large towns, with fields between extending from one to another, was pleasant." The Indians were anything but pleasant. They harassed de Soto constantly and he continued westward into what is now the state of Mississippi. Finally in the spring of 1541, his army exhausted and hungry, he reached the Mississippi River, south of present-day Memphis.

The Spaniards were profoundly impressed by the brown torrent of what they called the Great River. According to one chronicle of the expedition, the river was so wide that "a man standing on the shore could not be told, whether he were a man or something else, from the other side. The stream was swift, and very deep; the water, always flowing turbidly, brought along from above many trees and much timber, driven onward by its force." It would be several centuries before the true dimensions of this mighty river system would be known. The Mississippi-Missouri is the third longest in the world, being exceeded only by the Nile and the Amazon. Each year it carries to its mouth more than 400 million tons of silt and debris, enough material to cover Rhode Island to a depth of nearly three inches. Much of this material is deposited at the great river's mouth, where it has built up an extensive delta; in fact, most of the present land of Louisiana and Mississippi has been formed by the constant depositing of sediments stripped from the heartland of the continent by the Mississippi and its tributaries. Throughout much of its route south of Memphis the river constantly shifts its course, and it is entirely possible that the land on which de Soto stood to view the river is now under its waters.

The chronicle further relates that de Soto "went to look at the river, and saw that near it there was much timber of which boats might be made." No trees were mentioned by name, but several species of the lower Mississippi are particularly prominent. In addition to the live oaks, he must have noted the great beeches of the swamp forest and the gigantic sycamores with their scaly white trunks and branches. In later times, river boat pilots trying to follow the meandering course of the stream at night used the whiteness of sycamores growing along the banks as beacons.

After crossing the Mississippi in boats made on the spot, de Soto found nim-self in a morass of swamps and oxbow bends, his men marching "through water, in places coming to the knees; in others, as high as the waist." As they floundered in the mud, they declared it "the worst tract for swamp and water that they had found." But they were greatly impressed by the fishes, the huge Mississippi catfish unlike any they had seen before: "the third part of which was head, with gills from end to end, and along the sides were great spines, like very sharp awls." They reported that some weighed 150 pounds; indeed in the old days 100-pounders were often caught in the Mississippi.

The most unusual fish they encountered was the paddlefish, a living fossil which has a skeleton of cartilage similar to that of another group of ancient fishes, the sharks of the ocean. Only two species of paddlefish survive on the planet, one in the Mississippi and the other in the rivers of China. De Soto's men caught one in a net and described it as without scales, "the snout a cubit in length, the upper lip being shaped like a shovel." This flat, paddlelike snout —which may be a third as long as its body—is its most distinctive feature. No one knows for certain its function. It is thought by some scientists that it may be used to dip up the mud of the river bottom in search of food; others hold it is a sensory organ for detecting the presence of food, or even a stabilizer for its long body. As recently as the end of the last century, specimens six feet in length and weighing nearly 200 pounds were taken from the Mississippi, but those caught today are much smaller. Intensive fishing is probably not the real explanation for its decline; rather, the building of dams on the upper river is believed to have altered the sand and gravel bottoms downstream which are this fish's preferred spawning sites.

Once across the Mississippi, de Soto turned west to the Boston Mountains, still led on by rumors of gold, but these proved no more accurate than other rumors he had already traced across half a continent. Still he kept relentlessly on, pushing almost to the Arkansas-Oklahoma border. There the futility of his quest finally caught up with him. There was no gold, no Seven Cities, no route to the South Seas. The spring of 1542 found him encamped miserably on the Arkansas River, near where it joins the Mississippi. Needing reinforcements, he sent a scouting party south to make contact with a small Spanish fleet sup-posedly cruising along the Gulf coast. But the scouts never got there; they foundered in another endless bog. In May of that year, de Soto succumbed to a "putrid fever." After another futile foray westward, the remnants of his force, clothed in deerskin, set to work building boats. They sailed down the Mis-sissippi to the Gulf, turned west and then south, following the coast all the way to the vicinity of Tampico, Mexico.

ONLY 311 half-starved and bedraggled men of an original force of 600 final-ly reached the little village in Mexico. Although they returned empty-handed, they brought with them a richness in knowledge that was quickly trans-mitted to Europe. Revised maps of the continent were drawn and a whole new concept of its majestic dimensions emerged—for the expedition had passed through some 350,000 square miles of North America, explored from Florida northward to the Carolinas, traveled on the prairies almost as far north as the Missouri River, discovered the Mississippi and floated down it to its delta.

De Soto and his men had been too busy trying to survive to make much more than passing observations about the natural history of the country through which they marched. For more than two centuries it went almost undescribed,

TWO SWIMMING RELICS

Left over from the Permian, the pad-dlefish (above) and the bowfin (below) have existed almost unchanged in Amer-ican rivers for 230 million years and are still found in the Mississippi. Seldom weighing more than 50 pounds now, or about a third its previous known size, the paddlefish uses its gaping, paddle-topped mouth to engulf fresh-water shrimp, small aquatic insects and other food strained from the water by gill rak-ers. The 10-pound male bowfin, which is marked by a yellow circle near the tail, fiercely protects its young fry, as seen be-low, until they are about a month old. The bowfin is hated by sportsmen be-cause it eats game fish and does not taste good itself, but paddlefish eggs are some-times passed off by restaurants as caviar.

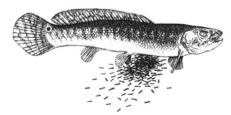

except for occasional details from the settlers who were beginning to filter into it. Fortunately for those wishing to reconstruct a picture of wilderness America, much of de Soto's route was retraced or approximated by the travels between 1773 and 1778 of William Bartram of Philadelphia, one of North America's early naturalists. Fortunately, too, Bartram traveled just as the southeastern wilderness was about to be tamed. He recorded for posterity much about primeval America—but he also saw the lofty pine forest being leveled, a wolf pup killed by being beaten over the head with a gun stock, bears that were still fearless of man being senselessly shot along with their cubs.

BARTRAM's account of his travels fills in many curious omissions in the chronicles of de Soto's expedition. Most curious, perhaps, is de Soto's failure to mention the continent's big alligators, although these animals were abundant in most of the regions he explored. To Bartram, they were a major ingredient of the landscape, and he gives a vivid, if somewhat melodramatic, description of a large Florida alligator: "Behold him rushing forth from the flags and reeds. His enormous body swells. His plaited tail, brandished high, floats upon the lake. The waters like a cataract descend from his opening jaws. Clouds of smoke issue from his dilated nostrils. The earth trembles with his thunder." The concentrations of alligators that Bartram encountered in Florida may never again be seen on the continent: "in such incredible numbers and so close together from shore to shore that it would have been easy to have walked across on their heads." Bartram recorded that some of these specimens reached the prodigious length of 20 feet. For about 150 years this length was regarded as a wild exaggeration—until an alligator shot in Louisiana was found to measure 19 feet, 2 inches. No such gigantic specimens remain today, for the adult alligator has been persistently hunted for its hide. Young ones were also captured for sale as pets—with the result that alligators are nowhere numerous now, except in a few places like Everglades National Park.

De Soto was also unaccountably silent about the venomous snakes. They are all still common in the southern lowlands, and 400 years ago they must have swarmed there in countless numbers. Particularly conspicuous are the pit vipers—the copperhead, water moccasin and rattlesnake. The Spaniards must have seen these, and when they did, they probably took them for European vipers, to which they bear considerable similarity. They are, in fact, closely related, both groups having long hypodermiclike venom fangs that are folded back in the mouth when not in use. However, there is one significant difference between the two families. The pit vipers bear that name not because, as some people think, they live in depressions in the ground but because they have nostril-like holes, or "pits," in their faces. These represent an evolutionary advance over the European vipers, but their function was not understood until 1937, when experiments revealed that the pits were sensory equipment for the location of warm-blooded prey. These snakes, in short, do everything that an ordinary viper can do in the way of striking and poisoning small mammals and birds, but they can also do it in pitch-darkness.

The pit vipers have all undergone considerable evolutionary radiation in North America, particularly the rattlers, which are often considered to occupy the highest rung on the snakes' evolutionary ladder. Rattlesnakes are found only in the New World, and in North America they come in a variety of sizes from the relatively primitive pygmy rattler, with its small rattle and puny venom supply, to the huge southern species that have very large rattles and venom glands, highly developed sensory equipment and complex behavior patterns.

It may seem odd that the rattler cannot hear its own rattle. It has no ears and can only detect sounds of extremely low frequency through the vibrations they make in the ground. Otherwise, snakes are deaf—and it may well be asked why they ever developed rattles. The answer is that the rattling sound is not aimed at snakes at all, but at other animals. Rattlers seem to have evolved in North America during the Middle Tertiary, at a time when many hoofed mammals —rhinoceroses, horses, camels and other forms that later became extinct in North America—were also developing. It is unlikely that a rattlesnake bite would have been enough to kill one of these large animals; still it must have been extremely painful, and it can be assumed that any animal that stepped on a buzzing snake once and got an excruciating bite probably learned to avoid that noise the next time it heard it—much as a bird learns to avoid the black-and-yellow warning stripes on stinging wasps. In this way natural selection probably played its part in the evolution of the rattle, since the snakes with the loudest noisemakers had the best chance of not being stepped on and hence of living long enough to reproduce themselves. Today, over a dozen species of rattlesnakes inhabit a wide range of environments in North America, with numerous subspecies grading almost imperceptibly into each other across the continent. Despite occasional local abundance, their numbers are considerably reduced, not only because of the changes in their habitat wrought by European man but also because of the constant persecution they have undergone. Apparently the largest of all rattlesnakes, the eastern diamondback of the southern states, was already declining in Bartram's time, for he wrote: "I have heard of their having been seen formerly, at the first settling of Georgia, seven, eight, and even ten feet in length . . . but there are none of that size to be seen now."

A RATTLER'S RATTLE

The rattle with which the rattlesnake warns of its presence is formed by loosely interlocking hollow rings of hard skin left after each molt, which make a buzzing sound when shaken. In the picture shown here, the snake, as a baby, began to form its rattles with the button at the very tip of its tail. Thereafter, with each successive molt, a new ring was formed. Popular belief holds that a snake's age can be told by counting the rings, but this is fallacious—a snake may molt as often as four times a year; also rattles tend to wear or break off with time.

BARTRAM also wrote eloquently of the open sky of the southland, through which flew hosts of birds—some now greatly diminished, others completely absent. One, the whooping crane, is no longer found in Florida; in fact it had vanished from that state even before Bartram was there. Today the entire world population of this species—about 30 birds at this writing—winters in a sanctuary on the Gulf coast of Texas and breeds in northwestern Canada. This stately white crane, standing five feet in height, is one of the rarest birds on the continent. Not very plentiful at the time European man arrived, it went into a sudden and drastic decline as it was shot for sport and for food, and its breeding grounds drained. In wilderness America, it had wintered along the Gulf coast from Florida to Mexico and on the Atlantic seaboard as far north as New Jersey. But it rapidly became virtually unknown east of the Mississippi River. The last record of its having nested south of Canada was a lone report made by an observer in Iowa in 1894.

The whooping crane has been the subject of one of the most dedicated attempts ever made to preserve a bird species from extinction, yet during the last half century its population has never gone above 50 birds. Its wintering grounds on the Texas coast have been set aside as the Aransas National Wildlife Refuge, and the discovery of its breeding grounds in Wood Buffalo Park, Canada, in 1954 has led to protection there also. Twice each year, as the birds migrate between Aransas and Wood Buffalo Park, bird watchers and sportsmen alike alert the public to give the cranes safe passage. It is likely that no one shoots at the great cranes now, yet the birds have failed to make a dramatic recovery, and hopes that their loud whoop will long continue to rend the air are bleak.

One reads with wonder and envy about the richness of bird life observed by Bartram. Of the smaller, more numerous sandhill crane he wrote: "The music of the seraphic cranes resounds in the skies; in separate squadrons they sail, encircling their precincts." Although the sandhill cranes still are present in Florida, their ranks have been thinned considerably and "squadrons" of them assuredly no longer exist. One is amazed to read his description of a vulture: "The bare skin on the neck appears loose and wrinkled and is of a deep bright-yellow color, intermixed with coral red. The hinder part of the neck is nearly covered with short, stiff hair; and the skin of part of the neck is of a dun-purple color, gradually becoming red as it approaches the yellow of the sides and fore part." Although Bartram called it "the painted vulture," so precise is the description that it could be no other bird but the king vulture of Central and South America. Bartram is the only person ever to have reported this bird from Florida, and some have questioned the accuracy of his sighting. Nevertheless, other species have given impressive evidence of how rapidly a bird can decline after the arrival of European man, and there is now little doubt that Florida must once have been within the range of this magnificent bird.

O NE other southeastern bird abundant in Bartram's day—the ivory-billed woodpecker—is kept on the roster of extant species more out of sentiment than hard facts, since no published sightings of it have been made since the early 1950s. It is hoped, although there is little evidence, that a few birds may still survive in remote areas of northern Florida and eastern Texas. The ivory-bill was the largest woodpecker in the world, except for the imperial woodpecker of Mexico, and it once was found in river-valley forests from the Carolinas to Florida, then westward in the forests that lined the rivers flowing into the Gulf of Mexico. Its habitat was described by Audubon in 1830: "Deep morasses, overshadowed by millions of gigantic dark cypresses, spreading their sturdy moss-covered branches. . . . Would that I could represent to you the dangerous nature of the ground, its oozing, spongy and miry disposition. . . ." This wilderness world of the virgin swamps was soon to disappear, and with it went the ivory-bill. Hunting no doubt lessened its numbers, but the real reason for the decline lies in the cutting down of the bottomland forests. The ivory-bill possessed an adaptation which in primeval times no doubt aided it in avoiding competition with other woodpeckers, but with the coming of European man this adaptation led to the bird's downfall. It lived on a specialized insect diet of wood-boring larvae that tunnel under the bark of trees that have been dead for two to three years. Trees meeting these exact requirements were necessarily rare, and thus the ivory-bill required extensive areas in which to live and breed. When the lumbermen cut their way across the southland, the giant woodpecker's doom was sealed.

Today the southern lowlands are the scene of a massive tree-planting and forest-conservation effort. Lumbermen who used to "cut out and get out" today are planting pines by the millions, but they are rebuilding only a semblance of the pristine southern forest. The trunks of pines stretch in sentinel rows as far as the eye can see. But this forest can never be more than a shadow of the destroyed one. Not only are particular species gone forever but the entire web of relationships built up over thousands of years has been ripped apart. And if the modern science of forestry cannot rebuild for us today even a pine forest, consider how much more difficult it would be to re-create the endless complexity of a primeval cypress swamp.

DAMSELFLIES MATE ON A BRANCH IN A COASTAL SWAMP. THEIR OFFSPRING WILL LIVE THREE OR FOUR YEARS IN WATER BEFORE ADULTHOOD

A Land beyond the Shore

The swamps behind the beaches and islands along much of North America's eastern shore form a strange and unique world. Although no swamp is typical of this widely diverse coast, the marshlands of South Carolina's Cape Romaine, shown on the following pages, are an excellent case study. They proceed inland in definite stages, each with its distinctive wildlife and geological history.

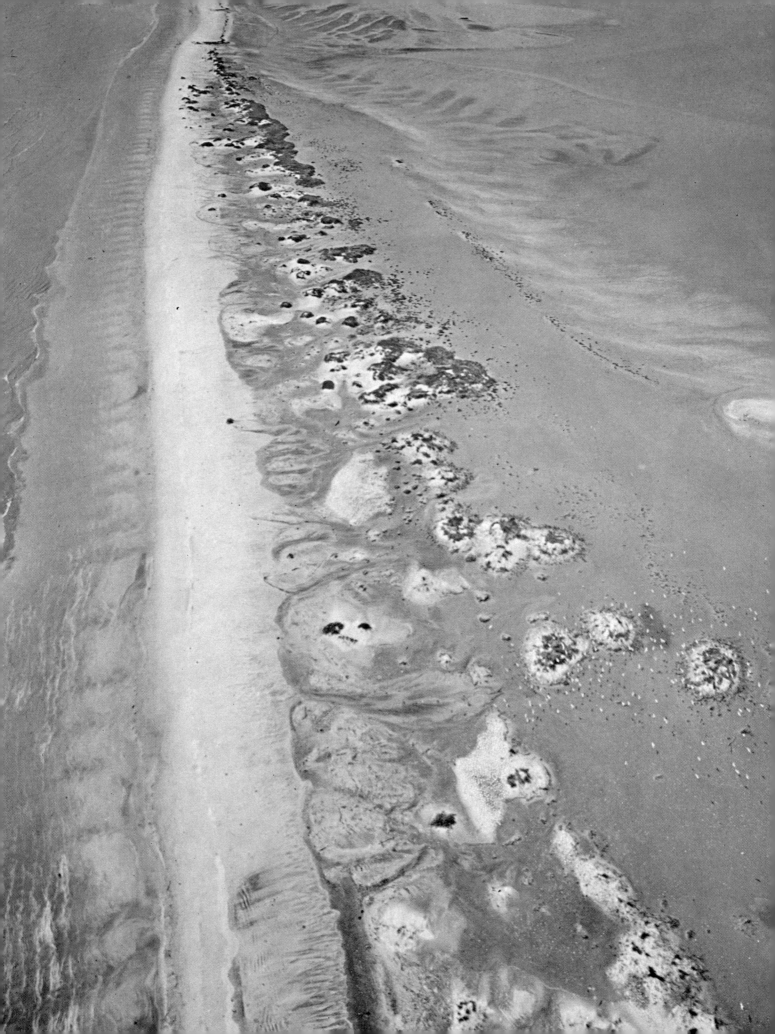

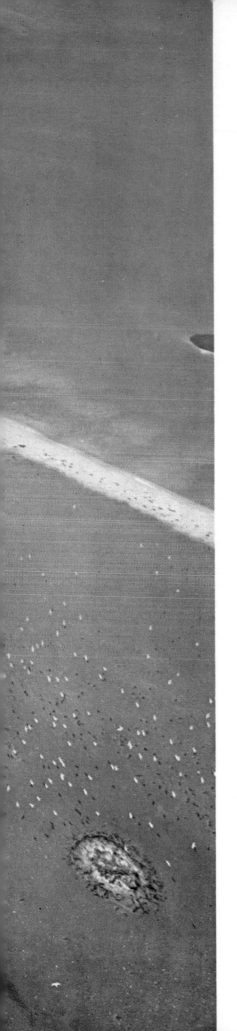

BROWN PELICANS, the smallest in the pelican family, nest near Cape Romaine. Adult pelicans, about six feet in wing span, feed their screaming nestlings with fish from the lagoon.

A Wall against the Sea

Along the eastern shore of North America, from Texas to New Jersey, a great chain of long, narrow islands lies parallel to the coast. These are the barrier beaches, dredged up from the ocean floor by heavy storm waves that pile immense quantities of sand above the normal level of the waves, leaving a protected lagoon on the lee side. Windswept and barren, the barrier beaches are a harsh environment, and except for a few hardy rodents, mammals are almost nonexistent there. Birds, however, breed and roost there by the millions, feeding on insects, fish and small marine creatures. Among the few plants that grow in the infertile sand is the sea oat, a tall, handsome grass that closely resembles its landlocked namesake. Its long, spidery roots allow it to extract what little nourishment the sand may offer—a delicate balance of rainfall and mineral nutrients from the sea— and the roots also bind the sand tightly, helping to form and maintain dunes. If a river flows into the lagoon behind, the beach may form a protective sea wall for an utterly different environment: the salt-water lagoon may be transformed into a brackish reservoir, or if the river is laden with mud, the sediment will slowly build up until a coastal swamp is formed.

SEEN FROM THE AIR, the barrier beach in places seems to merge with the sea, which beats upon it from the left; but its grassbound dunes offer a refuge to thousands of royal terns.

A SODDEN STRIP between land and sea, South Carolina's coastal marshes occupy a ribbon of land that rarely exceeds 10 miles in width. Such salt marshes can build up behind other shelters than barrier beaches—those shown here formed behind the Sea Islands, remnants of prehistoric hills protruding from the sea along the coast from Georgia to North Carolina. An outstanding bird sanctuary, the area harbors many species; canvasback ducks breed and winter by the thousands, feasting on a bonanza of mollusks and minuscule swamp creatures that abound in the area. This entire region is known by geologists as the Pamlico terrace, the lowest and youngest of seven such terraces in South Carolina. Caused by the intermittent rise and fall of the coastline, the terraces could be compared to a giant stairway marching out of the sea almost to the fall line far inland. About 100,000 years ago the Pamlico terrace was high and dry, and rivers carved out shallow hills and valleys. Then the land sank into the sea, leaving only the old hilltops exposed. There is evidence that the coast is still sinking at the rate of a few feet each century; in fact, scientists have discovered an ancient sandy beach far offshore, in 300 feet of water.

BEHIND THE MARSHES is a 50-mile-wide zone of savannas and fresh-water swamps. In prehistoric times this region was a seashore, but it is now many miles inland and as much as 130 feet above sea level in some places. As the land rose, barrier beaches, created one after the other by the receding sea, left a phalanx of ridges roughly parallel to the coast. Drainage from the area is poor; luxuriant vegetation has clogged many of the waterways, and so numerous bays and swamps have formed. Countless unnamed rivers wind their way through a tortuous series of loops and curlicues before they finally reach the ocean. When settlers came, they found the swamps were ideal for growing rice and introduced the crop in 1686, razing immense areas of virgin forest in the process. South Carolina produced more than half of the rice output of the United States until the Civil War. But during the conflict the crops were neglected, and afterward, without slave labor, the fields could not be worked profitably. The state's last attempt at commercial rice production was in 1926. Now the old rice paddies are blanketed by strong young forests of long-leaf pine and oak, and the wilderness has, for the time being, emerged victorious.

LONG-LEAF PINES, growing on sandy lowlands bordering the marshes, emerge as terminal buds *(top)*. Only after a substantial root network has spread do they shoot up, perhaps as high as 120 feet *(bottom)*.

A CANEBRAKE RATTLER coils itself into striking position. Brother to the timber and banded rattlers, *Crotalus horridus atricaudatus* is one of the swamp's most dangerous creatures which, full-grown, may reach a length of eight feet.

CYPRESS AND DUCKWEED blanket the edge of an upland lake. Although the cypress bears cones and belongs to the same family as the evergreen pines, it sheds its leaves each year.

The Upland Cypress Swamps

Above the brackish swamps of the South Carolina coast lie the barrens, a region of rolling coniferous forest punctuated with fresh-water lakes and cypress swamps. The shallow valleys of this upland country are regularly flooded by spring rains, but drainage is much better than in the lowlands, and the earth is nearly dry for several months a year. Here, combined with relatively mild winters, is the perfect environment for bald cypress trees, since mature trees can live almost indefinitely in water but the cypress seedlings can take root only on dry land.

THE SNAKELIKE NECK of an anhinga thrusts above water as it gulps a fish. It spears a fish with its long sharp beak, tosses it into the air and swallows it head first.

SPECTACULAR RESIDENT of cypress swamps, the water-loving anhinga has a strange problem: its feathers absorb water. After a swim, it must spread its wings to dry.

The Bellowing Alligator

The largest reptile in North America is the alligator, a latter-day saurian that haunts rivers and swamps from North Carolina to Mexico. The only other alligators in the world live in China, and these are much smaller than their American relatives. Before hunters began to slaughter them by the thousands, large numbers of these members of the order Crocodilia were a familiar sight in the southern lowlands. Now they are fairly well restricted to a few remote areas where they are protected both by isolation and by stringent game laws. The alligator is the only reptile with a loud voice—its bellows can be heard for more than a mile away. When a male bellows, he emits a potent jet of musky vapor that leaves no doubt as to his whereabouts—probably a method of establishing territory during the mating season. Al-

A RARE PHOTOGRAPH CATCHES A FEMALE ALLIGATOR LAYING HER EGGS. TO BUILD HER NEST, SHE GATHERED A LARGE PILE OF VEGETATION AND

though it is a fearsome creature when it is dealing with its fellow animals, the alligator is almost embarrassingly timid when it encounters a man—unless it is cornered, in which case it can be exceedingly dangerous. It can close its jaws with enough force to crush a man's leg. Curiously enough, the muscles that open its jaws are so weak that a man can hold a full-grown alligator's mouth closed with one hand.

THE BABY ALLIGATOR, black with sharp yellow stripes, gradually turns a uniform gray or dirty black as it grows older.

PACKED IT DOWN WITH HER BODY. WHEN SHE FINISHES LAYING, SHE WILL CAREFULLY COVER THE EGGS WITH A LAYER OF DECAYING VEGETATION

5

The Great Eastern Forests

ALTHOUGH the early explorers examined the timber of the New World in the professional light of its potential for ships' masts and planking, a genuine awe of the great eastern forests seems to penetrate their descriptions. "The woods . . . are thick with the highest and reddest cedars in the world, far better than the cedars of the Azores, of the Indies, or of Lebanon," claimed one account. Another voyager was impressed by the "stately timber," and he catalogued "fir, birch, oak, and beech, as far as we saw along the shore. . . . Upon the hills grow notable high timber trees." Not only were the trees impressive but the whole luxuriance of the forest community: Verrazano commented on the "wild roses, violets, and lilies, and many sorts of herbs and fragrant flowers different from ours."

Before the lumberman's ax rang throughout the eastern forests, they lay like a green blanket across the eastern United States and a portion of southeastern Canada. But these forests are forever gone; a shadowy glimpse of their original character can be obtained only by studying the few isolated pockets of primeval woods that survive today. The most extensive portion that escaped being ravaged by European man is the forest of the Great Smoky Mountains. Now protected as a national park, the mountains are densely carpeted with green from base to summit, giving us some idea of what the entire eastern part of the continent must once have looked like. Nearly 20 kinds of North American trees reach record proportions in the Smokies; there are more species found in this small area than grow native in all of Europe. These remnant pockets, as well as the accounts of early travelers, indicate that the eastern forests stretched from the evergreen belt of Canada southward to the Gulf coastal plain, covering a third of the continent from the Atlantic westward beyond the Mississippi River as far as the Ozark Mountains. Most of this area was dominated by the deciduous species that are leafless in winter, although evergreen white pines and hemlocks grew in the northern portion, loblolly and pitch pines in the southern. All together, it contained approximately 130 species of trees in numerous combinations—usually oaks, hickories and sugar maple on dry slopes or uplands; red maple and elms in lower areas; willows and sycamores along streams.

B ECAUSE of their great size the eastern forests have been the subject of a myth that is perpetuated to this day—"vast, continuous . . . dim and silent as a cavern" in the words of the 19th Century traveler and historian Francis Parkman. It has been said that a squirrel could have traveled from bough to bough for a thousand miles without ever touching ground. But this concept of an unbroken forest is clearly an exaggeration. It overlooks the effect upon it of the woodland Indian tribes, particularly the Iroquoian and Algonquian, which drew upon the forest bounty for village sites and crop fields, for wooden weapons and canoes, for medicines from tree roots. An Iroquoian village site often covered as much as 150 acres of cleared forest land; hundreds of them have already been found by archeologists, and the sites no doubt numbered in the thousands. Beyond the villages and fields, the forests were constantly culled in an endless search for firewood, and even farther away from the village sites, Indians burned large areas to clear trails and to drive out game. So thoroughly had the forests around Boston been leveled by Indians that the colonists had to sail to islands in the harbor to find firewood.

Although our vision of continuous forest is no doubt a romanticized one, nevertheless in its primeval state it must have been an impressive sight. Its profusion of plant life offered numerous feeding niches and shelter for a rich array of animal inhabitants. All of these have declined except for a few kinds. The raccoon and opossum have succeeded in adapting to the new man-dominated environment. And for some, the cutting of the forest has been a boon. These beneficiaries include deer, woodchucks, red foxes, cottontail rabbits and many songbirds; all are animals of the forest edge, and clearing and logging has multiplied the land available for them. There are today undoubtedly many more songbirds inhabiting the area once covered by the eastern forests than there were at the discovery of the continent. But, for most animal species, the presence of European man in the forests has led to a drastic decline. The numbers of some animals, such as gray squirrels, have probably fallen simply because there is less forest land for them. For others—hawks and owls, black bears, bobcats, beavers—an additional important cause of decline has been direct overhunting or persecution by man. And for a few the story is one of complete extirpation. The mountain lion was once probably the commonest large carnivore of the eastern forests, but it is now virtually extinct in the east except for Mississippi, Louisiana and Florida, and an occasional unconfirmed report from New Brunswick or Maine. A bison cow and her calf killed in West Virginia in 1825 represent the

AN END OF EMIGRATION

One of the extraordinary natural phenomena that disappeared with the decline of the eastern forests was the occasional mass emigration of the gray squirrel. Caused by an excessive build-up of their populations, these movements involved millions of the animals—a half-billion were estimated to have migrated across southern Wisconsin in 1843. Moving in hordes, they devoured crops, and even though they are poor swimmers, they nevertheless struggled across such mighty rivers as the Ohio (above), thousands drowning in the effort. Today, the squirrel population, although smaller, is currently on the increase; emigrations still occur but they are not often noticeable.

last record of this animal east of the Mississippi; elk persisted in Pennsylvania until 1867 but are now found nowhere in the eastern woods except where reintroduced in recent years; wolves survived until the present century but are now gone; the caribou have retreated northward.

White-tailed deer, however, have found the altered landscape a boon. Originally they must have subsisted mainly at the edge of forest clearings or in burnt-over areas, since the tender buds and low growth on which they feed are either scarce or unreachable in mature forests. Heavily hunted by the Indians, then later senselessly slaughtered by the Europeans, deer quickly became so reduced that as early as 1696 Massachusetts had to declare a closed season. By the time of the American Revolution every colony except Georgia had laws prohibiting deer hunting. In 1763, a French explorer wrote: "When we discovered this vast Continent, it was full of Deer . . . But a Handful of Frenchmen have within a single Age found Means to make them almost entirely disappear." But the regeneration of so much forest and the subsequent sprouting of low growth in the last century have allowed the whitetail to extend its range. It is probably the most abundant large mammal in the United States today: although nearly a million are shot each year, their total population is believed to exceed six million.

What is commonly called "deer" in North America refers, in fact, to two species—the white-tailed deer and the mule deer—although the elk, moose and caribou are also members of the same family. All are hoofed animals that shed their antlers each year. Whitetails are found in much of the continent from the coniferous forest southward, the most notable exceptions being most of California and the Great Basin. The mule deer, or black-tailed deer, lives chiefly in the forests and brushy areas in the west. The elk, moose and caribou are such comparative newcomers from Asia that they have changed little from similar Eurasian species, but the whitetail's ancestor obviously made an early arrival in North America, millions of years ago. There are now more than 20 North American subspecies or races, including the miniature Key deer of Florida.

TODAY the whitetail is a commonplace in the North American landscape. We are likely to forget that, had it remained rare, people would travel hundreds of miles and wait patiently in forest glades with field glasses poised merely to catch a glimpse of this lissome, splendidly antlered animal. For sheer grace of movement, few mammals can equal the whitetail. It has been clocked at nearly 35 miles an hour, and it appears able to sustain a speed of 25 for several miles without flagging. Claims for its high jumping and broad jumping ability seem exaggerated, but actual measurements have shown them to be true. A running jump of 29 feet and the clearing of eight-and-a-half-foot-high obstacles have been recorded. Even a fawn possesses what has been described as "the very embodiment of graceful form and agile motion"; when only a few weeks old it is already agile enough to evade capture by a human.

During the time that predatory mountain lions and wolves still roamed the eastern forests, they undoubtedly made deep inroads upon the deer population. Today the main predators besides man are dogs, and to a small extent bobcats. Bobcats and deer live in much the same sort of forest habitat, and although the former may weigh no more than 25 pounds, it can bring down a 200-pound buck by getting its fangs into the deer's neck and holding on with its claws. This is usually possible only in deep snow, which fatally handicaps the deer. The American colonists were much impressed with this little relative of the mountain lion, and one contemporary description stated: "This Cat is quite different from those in Europe. . . . He takes most of his Prey by Surprize, getting up the Trees which they pass by or under, and thence leaping directly upon them. Thus he takes Deer (which he cannot catch by running) and fastens his Teeth into their Shoulders and sucks them."

The bobcat in many ways resembles a large tomcat, except for its very short tail. It is found throughout much of the United States and down into Mexico, but it penetrates only a short distance up into Canada where, in the coniferous forests and tundra, it is replaced by its larger relative, the Canada lynx. Bobcats were probably plentiful in the eastern forests in the early years of discovery, for the Catskill Mountains of New York received their name from Henry Hudson who called them Kaatskill ("Wildcat Creek") Mountains. The bobcat is still a widespread animal, but it has grown exceptionally wary of man and seldom ventures forth in daylight; few people realize that it is present in many settled areas. When cornered, it is ferocious—screaming, spitting, hissing and lashing out with its sharp claws; a single hunting dog is rarely able to overpower it. Even when caught in a trap, the bobcat has been known to fight off a coyote. The pioneer who boasted that he could lick his weight in wildcats was setting an impossible standard for himself.

In the ebb and flow of animal populations in the great eastern forests since their invasion by man, another animal that has been able to adjust, and to even extend its range, is the opossum, traditionally an inhabitant of the more southeastern forests. This strange animal is quite unlike any known in Europe, and early viewers were considerably confused as to exactly what it was. One Englishman wrote in 1616: "The Opassum hath a head like a Swine, a tayle like a Rat, as big as a Cat, and hath under her belly a bag, wherein she carrieth her young. . . . It hath the bodie of a Fox, handed and footed like a Monkey." The opossum is the only North American marsupial—a mammal which possesses an external pouch in which its young are carried. The babies crawl into the pouch immediately after birth and attach themselves to their mother's nipples. The first Europeans to see the opossum supposed that the young were born in the pouch—and one theory even stated that they did not develop in the womb at all but rather grew on the female's nipples until they were large enough to break off. This mistaken idea no doubt arose from the fact that the infant is permanently attached for the first 40 days of its life; the nipple enlarges in its mouth and the two are fastened as with a ball-and-socket joint.

THE opossum presents a strange anomaly of mammalian survival. It can trace back its ancestry in North America for some 80 million years, further than any other living mammal. Until about 25 million years ago, these pouched animals thrived in North America and in South America also, which they reached via temporary land bridges. They diversified into at least 30 genera in North and South America, but all of the North American ones died out, presumably in the face of competition from more advanced placental mammals. The single species that exists here today is a reinvader from South America. It is believed to have come back over the Central American land bridge after the latter rose a few million years ago. The opossum would appear, at first glance, to be an unlikely candidate for survival. It is not a capable fighter, a particularly agile climber or a fast runner. Its brain is only about a fourth as big as a house cat's, although the two animals have about the same body size; moreover, the structure of its brain lacks complex centers of learning ability and memory. Finally, it must depend on the marsupial pattern of reproduction and development, long assumed to be less efficient than that of the placental mammals, where the young are sheltered inside the mother.

Obviously these drawbacks to survival are illusions, for the opossum does survive, so successfully that within the present century it has extended its range from southern New York State through much of New England north into Canada, and west as far as Minnesota. For one thing, it possesses a behavioral pattern of being able to "play possum." This, combined with its apparently unpalatable taste, results in low predation pressure. Second, the marsupial pattern of reproduction is probably not so inefficient as it appears. Although it is true that there is a high mortality of young animals at birth, the litters are very large, and the female's ability to rear two litters a year gives the opossum a high reproductive potential. Finally, and perhaps most important, the opossum has never become highly specialized, either in structure or in habits, as have the marsupial kangaroos of Australia. It can make use of almost any dark hole as a den; its food consists of a wide range of fruits and berries, and nearly any kind of animal matter, living or dead; and whenever it finds itself in competition with more efficient placental mammals, it can switch over to a different food or habitat. The opossum one sees today is essentially a larger version of its ancestors of 80 million years ago. Its sole obvious specialization is a prehensile tail which can act as a fifth hand in the trees.

Possibly the only other forest mammal whose ancient genealogy and widespread distribution can approach that of the opossum is the raccoon, distinguished by its bandit's face mask and conspicuously ringed tail. The raccoon is nearly transcontinental in range and occurs from southern Canada to Central America. It early attracted the attention of the colonists, and soon fantastic tales of its peculiarities began to appear. It was accounted "the drunkenest creature living, if he can get any Liquour that is sweet and strong." This alleged drunkenness probably stems from the raccoon's marked taste for sweets and apples, and the colonists combined both in apple cider. Few bits of folklore about the raccoon have clung so tenaciously as the belief that it washes its food before eating; in fact, its scientific species name of *lotor* means "washer." Actually the raccoon makes no attempts in particular to wash its food. It preys often upon water animals—crayfish, mussels, fish and frogs—and as a result may be seen with its paws dipped in water.

Another animal originally abundant throughout the forested regions of the continent, the beaver, was exploited for its fur far more than the opossum or the raccoon. In fact, much of the early exploration into the interior of the continent is due to the quest for beaver pelts. At the time that beaver hats went out of fashion, by the beginning of the 19th Century, the animal was virtually extinct east of the Mississippi River. A dire prediction was made at that time that "the race will eventually be extinguished throughout the whole continent. A few individuals may, for a time, elude the immediate violence of persecution, and like the degraded descendants of the aboriginals of our soil, be occasionally exhibited as melancholy mementos of tribes long previously whelmed in the fathomless gulf of avarice." This prediction has not come true; as in the case of the sea otter, fur seal, elk, gray whale and certain of the wading birds and waterfowl—all of which once trod the thin edge of extinction—the beaver has been restored to safe levels of survival because of the helping hand of wildlife conservationists. Once again the beaver is seen in the eastern forests, although the creeks and rivers are no longer full of them, as in the past, when large parts of Pennsylvania between Easton and the Pocono Mountains were turned into swamp by the profusion of their dams. Nevertheless, the North American beaver has fared much better than the European species, which is now rare.

The colonists were quick to notice the fascinating ways of the beaver and to launch the inevitable exaggerations of its behavior. These crept into print, and one writer, becoming extremely critical, accused another of collecting "all the fictions into which other writers on the subject have run, but has so greatly improved on them that little remains to be added to his account of the beaver beside a vocabulary of their language, a code of their laws, and a sketch of their religion." The beaver has long been exalted, along with the bee and the ant, as a paragon of intelligence and industry, but most of the anecdotes are untrue. Not only does it not slap its tail on the ground as a warning to other beavers before toppling a tree, but it cannot even make the tree fall in any particular direction. Most beaver-cut trees simply fall the way they happen to lean, and if the cut tree's branches become entangled with those of another tree, preventing its fall, it never occurs to the beaver to gnaw down the other tree also.

The true facts about beavers are really more remarkable than the folklore. Their persistent instinct is to modify their environment by building dams, and it is this proclivity that accounts for much of the interest in them. As soon as a beaver moves into a new area, it almost immediately sets to work chewing off saplings and inserting them, longitudinally with the current, in the bottom of a stream. These are secured with mud and stones scooped up from the bottom, and more sticks and debris are added, until the dam is high enough to hold back a pond of sufficient depth to satisfy the beaver. A new dam of a beaver family is usually quite modest in size, but as the years go by it will be enlarged and repaired by several generations of beavers and may reach an astonishing size—sometimes as much as 12 feet high and, in one dam near Three Forks, Montana, a length of 2,040 feet. The purpose of these additions is to keep the water level up and also make available more distant trees when the nearer ones have all been cut down. In addition to the main dam, the beaver usually constructs other hydraulic works, notably a network of canals whereby it can float logs to the pond. Most canals are less than 100 feet in length, but one in the Adirondack Mountains of New York was 654 feet long.

T HE pattern of sharp decline in numbers of an animal population after the arrival of Europeans holds true also for the most typical of North American birds, the wild turkey. There is some dispute as to how turkeys originated. Some zoogeographers think they are derived from ancient Asiatic pheasant-like stock, others do not. But all agree that turkeys—as turkeys—developed right here, one of the few families of living North American birds that can make that claim. It is difficult to estimate the primeval population of wild turkeys throughout the eastern forests, but it must have been huge. And the birds themselves may have been larger than the gobblers one finds today. Nowadays a 25-pounder is considered large, but there are tales of 50-pounders from colonial times. If there ever were such giants, an explanation for the larger size may be that in those days the wild turkeys were able to inhabit the most fertile parts of the forest where food was plentiful; today they have been forced back into the less fertile mountains.

At one time the wild turkey inhabited a tremendous range, from the New England woods southward as far as Florida and Mexico, and westward to the Mississippi River bottomlands, with isolated populations as far west as Arizona.

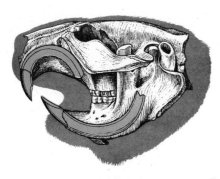

THE EVER-GROWING TEETH

Beavers need sharp teeth because they are constantly using them to gnaw down trees. And their large incisors (shown in color above) are kept sharp by having hard enamel faces and softer dentine backs. The dentine wears away faster than the enamel as the animal gnaws, leaving a keen biting edge of enamel at all times. Furthermore, these incisors never stop growing, so the beaver has to chew or grind its teeth continually to keep them ground down to a manageable length. If a beaver breaks a tooth or otherwise distorts its bite, the incisors elongate, force open the mouth permanently and cause the animal to starve.

But it has long disappeared from most of this range. As early as 1674 one traveler in New England wrote: "I have also seen three-score broods of young turkies on the side of a marsh, sunning of themselves in a morning betimes. But this was thirty years since; the English and the Indians having now destroyed the breed, so that 'tis very rare to meet with a wild turkie in the woods." The reasons for its decline are the familiar ones: destruction of habitat and overhunting. The cutting of the oak forests in many areas has much reduced the supply of winter food available to these nonmigratory birds; they have been hunted for food and for sport; and the disappearance of the fungus-blighted American chestnut has further depleted their food supply. For a good many years the remnant populations of wild turkeys have found refuge mainly in southern swamps and in a few remote areas in the eastern mountains. Today they are fanning out from these refuges and beginning to reclaim some of their lost domains, as abandoned farmlands in Pennsylvania and southern New York again sprout oak, beech and shagbark hickory. They are also being assisted by artificial transplanting of birds into areas where they once lived.

However, today's wild turkey is not the same bird that greeted the pioneers. In primeval North America, there were seven distinct races of this species. Two of them inhabited the eastern forests; two more were found from Texas to Arizona; there were three in Mexico itself, and it is the southernmost of these that was domesticated by the Aztecs. This Mexican bird was so highly regarded by the Spaniards that as early as 1526 it had become a popular domestic fowl in their West Indies colonies. Taken to Europe by the Spaniards, the bird was already appearing on menus in England in 1585. In due course it was reintroduced to the New World. Since the domesticated Mexican bird interbreeds readily with the wild eastern race, it is questionable to what extent the restocked "wild" turkeys of the east are truly wild or crosses with the Mexican race.

The English colonists in Virginia took early note of the abundant turkeys as well as other kinds of birds: "partridges" (probably grouse or bobwhite quail), "Black Birds with crimson wings" (the red-winged blackbird), and "divers sorts of small Birds, some read, some blew" (probably cardinals and bluebirds). They also found "Parrats and Pigeons" everywhere, but the woodswalker today sees only occasional doves and no parrots at all. The Carolina parakeet was among the most spectacular birds on the continent, judging by an early account: "most swift of wing, their winges and breast are of a greenish cullour, with forked tayles, their heads, some crymsen, some yellowe, some orange-tawny, very beautiful." The northernmost of the world's parrots, it was the only parrot to inhabit the United States, ranging as far north as New York State and west to the Dakotas. The last reliable sighting of a flock of wild parakeets was in 1920 near Fort Drum Creek in Florida, but rumors that some of these birds still lived in remote cypress swamps in South Carolina persisted until 1938, when all hope was finally abandoned. The last captive bird died in 1914. No indirect habitat changes account for the extirpation of the parakeets from the American landscape. Rather, their extinction is directly attributable to a variety of human factors. Farmers shot them because they destroyed fruit; plumage hunters killed them for their bright feathers; enormous numbers were trapped for the pet trade; finally, gunners shot them for mere sport. Like most other parrots, they had the habit of returning to the body of a shot member of the flock, thus making it easy for hunters to bag more of the flock than they killed with their first salvo.

The size of the passenger pigeon flocks seen by the colonists is almost unbelievable. One writer stated: "wild pigeons, in winter beyond number of imagination, myself have seen three or four hours together flocks in the air, so thick that even they have shadowed the sky from us." The ornithologist-artist Alexander Wilson observed a flock in about 1810 and calculated that it contained more than two billion birds. Audubon thought this an exaggeration and halved Wilson's estimate; even so, the more conservative figure still represents an incredible number of birds.

The passenger pigeons typified what appeared to be the limitless resources of the continent, and they fell before the hand of man in multitudes. In 1770 it was reported: "Some years past they have not been in such plenty as they used to be . . . everybody was amazed how few there were; and wondered at the reason." The reason was that many were killed because they fed on crops; in years when crops failed, they were killed for food. One way or another it was the passenger pigeon's fate to be killed, whether the year was one of feast or famine. There were less direct causes for the decline also—loss of nesting sites and food because of the cutting of the beech forests, and particularly, the birds' inability to live and breed successfully except in large flocks. An attempt in 1857 to limit the decimation of flocks in Ohio was turned down by the state legislature in the belief that no protection was necessary: "Wonderfully prolific, having the vast forests of the North as its breeding grounds, traveling hundreds of miles in search of food, it is here to-day and elsewhere to-morrow, and no ordinary destruction can lessen them or be missed from the myriads that are yearly produced." Actually the pigeons were not prolific; a pair of birds produced one squab a year or, if the first one failed, sometimes a second. What made them seem so was their fantastically large nesting colonies. Even during one of the last years of this species, there was a nesting site in Wisconsin more than 100 miles long and from six to eight miles wide. Nearly every tree in an area of about 800 square miles had nests in it, many of them had dozens of nests—tens of millions in all. What is still scarcely credible is that 30 years after this mass nesting the species would be extinct. The last definite record of a wild pigeon was a bird killed in Ohio in 1900, although sightings were reported for some years after that. One would like to think that the very last pigeon died as it had lived, in the free air above the Great Lakes forests or in the dark corridors of a remaining beech woods. But we know that the last one expired as a pitiful captive bird at the Cincinnati Zoo in September 1914—ironically in the same year that the last captive Carolina parakeet died.

T HE passenger pigeon is a symbol of man's wanton destruction—and also of the present-day determination that it shall never happen again. In 1947, the Wisconsin Society for Ornithology erected a monument to the extinct pigeon. At that time Aldo Leopold, the dedicated conservationist, observed: "We have erected a monument to commemorate the funeral of a species. It symbolizes our sorrow. We grieve because no living man will see again the onrushing phalanx of victorious birds, sweeping a path for spring across the March skies, chasing the defeated winter from all the woods and prairies of Wisconsin . . . For one species to mourn the death of another is a new thing under the sun. The Cro-Magnon who slew the last mammoth thought only of steaks. The sportsman who shot the last pigeon thought only of his prowess. The sailor who clubbed the last auk thought of nothing at all. But we, who have lost our pigeons, mourn the loss."

AUTUMN IN AMERICA'S WOODS IS A TIME OF MANY COLORS, WHEN SUNLIGHT AND COOL WEATHER TURN MAPLES TO FLAME AMONG CONIFERS

Survivors in the Woods

Two centuries ago, Elias Pym Fordham saw eastern North America as "nothing but an undulating surface of impenetrable forest." Today, civilization has left less than 25 per cent of the region in woodland, only one tenth of one per cent in primeval condition. Yet many of its original inhabitants survive there, ranging from the black bear and great horned owl to the ever-present woodchuck.

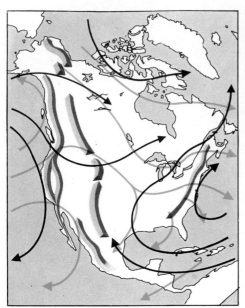

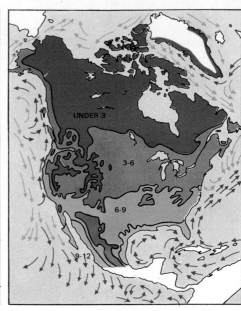

THE PREVAILING WINDS of winter (*blue*) are mostly westerlies, and those of summer (*black*) are tropical. The former drop moisture on the western ranges.

RAINFALL, heaviest in the Northwest, is shown in mean annual inches. The Great Plains, though fertile, get less rain or snow than the Southeast forest edge.

OCEAN CURRENTS, warm (*red*) or cold (*blue*), directly or indirectly affect the continent's growing seasons. Light areas show the longest, in frost-free months.

Wind, Weather and Biomes

Compact and well defined between the mountain ranges paralleling the coasts, the major biomes of North America are governed by a climate which is largely the product of two conflicting weather systems—that of the cold, dry Arctic and the hot, moist tropics. Since there is no transverse mountain barrier like that of the Himalayas in Asia, prevailing winds and rainfall are less variable the year round. In winter, ocean currents warm both coastlines but their effect is much lessened in the Northeast by prevailing cold winds from the interior. Thus, the heart of the deciduous forest, even though lying in the same latitude as the subtropical Mediterranean, has four distinct seasons and is far richer

in animal life than the coniferous forest of the north and the high western Rockies. Lower mountains in the Southwest, covered with woodlands of pine and oak, long ago were avenues through which gray fox, raccoon and mountain lion reached Central and South America. Along the Pacific coast, westerly winds bring varied degrees of moisture to local biomes ranging from chaparral to temperate rain forest. Beyond the mountains, the Great Basin is cold desert, characterized by sagebrush and jack rabbits, but in the Southwest hot deserts are as diverse as the creosote-and-lizard community of Death Valley, California, and Arizona saguaro cactus country, host to many birds, mammals and reptiles.

KEY

TUNDRA		CHAPARRAL
CONIFEROUS FOREST		WOODLAND
MOIST CONIFEROUS FOREST		SUBTROPICAL AND TROPICAL FOREST
TEMPERATE GRASSLANDS		HOT DESERT
TEMPERATE DECIDUOUS FOREST		COLD DESERT

Matt Greene

WAKE-ROBIN, SPRINGING FROM WET LEAF MOLD ON A ROCKY HILLSIDE, GLOWS IN THE APRIL SUN. LIKE OTHER TRILLIUMS, IT HAS SEPALS, PETALS, AND

A Calendar of Wildflowers

From Maine to Florida in the eastern woodlands, and westward to the Great Plains, multitudes of wildflowers—200 to 600 plants for every tree—provide a varied calendar of the growing season. Early bloomers, such as spring beauty, soon wither, but trilliums keep on growing under the canopy, to pro-

duce berries late in the summer. June is a burst of flowering shrubs, tapering off in July, when open meadows and glades are dotted with spiderworts and wild sunflowers. In the moist and shaded places, hardly any plant blooms until fringed gentians "bluer than the bluest sky" appear on the verge of frost.

SPIDERWORT—May-August

RUE ANEMONE—March-June

LEAVES ARRANGED IN THREES

MOUNTAIN LAUREL—May-July

PINK LADY'S SLIPPER—May-June

FRINGED GENTIAN—September-October

A YELLOWSTONE GRIZZLY, humped and huge, is one of the last few hundred left in western parks. Implanted with tiny radios, they are tracked to determine the range they need.

The Comeback of the Bears

To early Americans, Indians and settlers alike, bears were prime game—especially the plentiful black bear. Its hide was used for bedding and clothing, its rich meat for food, its fat for frying, fuel and healing ointment. Heavily hunted and beset in most of their eastern domain by forest-cutting, the large carnivores declined until 20th Century game laws gave them protection. Today, they are making a comeback wherever second-growth forest has reclaimed cultivated land; Pennsylvania, once populated by an estimated five bears per 10 square miles, today can support an average of two in the same area. Solitary and retiring, black bears make their homes in dense thickets as often as in large, old tree hollows, and their preferred foods, including berries, nuts, insects and small mammals, are as abundant in shrubbery and open, dry woodlots as in deep woods. In the Northwest and Rockies, where the less adaptable western grizzly is declining, hundreds of thousands of black bears still range over heavily logged and burned-over forests.

TREED IN A QUAKING ASPEN, A WESTERN BLACK BEAR LOOKS DOWN

ON ITS PURSUERS. SMALLER AND MORE AGILE THAN THE GRIZZLY, IT RUNS 32 MILES PER HOUR AND CLIMBS TREES IN A SERIES OF BOUNDS

A Dominant Predator

Noiseless as a flying shadow, the great horned owl is a predator that dominates the lives of an unusual number of woodland and field creatures. Because horned owls nest in January or February, a month before the largest hawks, they affect not only the populations of prey animals at the lower levels of the food pyramid but those of predators at the top as well. Young horned owls are fledged in about 12 weeks. To feed them during this long dependency, the parents take a heavy toll of their later-breeding neighbors, from small mammals, such as the pocket gopher, to the young and adults of hawks and smaller owls. In April, when snakes, frogs and crawfish come out of hibernation, they too become part of the young owls' diet. By July, when the fledgling owls are learning to hunt for themselves, large numbers of immature songbirds are on the wing, furnishing easy prey. And finally, in the fall and winter, the white-footed mice and cottontails, whose populations have built up under the protective summer ground cover, are conspicuous in the now barren woods, a dependable food supply in the lean seasons.

GNAWING ON A DISCARDED ANTLER, a white-footed mouse satisfies its craving for calcium and other minerals. Though meadow mice are 10 times as plentiful, the white-footed mice are more heavily preyed upon by owls in winter because they run over the snow in search of the saplings they feed on instead of tunneling safely below, as meadow mice generally do.

SNATCHED ON EMERGING FROM ITS HOLE, A POCKET GOPHER IS CARRIED OFF TO PROVIDE FOOD FOR YOUNG HORNED OWLS

DIGGING A DEN, the woodchuck loosens the earth with strong front claws and then *(below)* ejects stones and earth with its back ones.

CLEARING THE ENTRANCE *(below)*, the animal bulldozes stones away with its nose, preventing a landslide that would fill up its hole.

WOODCHUCK PAIRS HOLE UP TOGETHER FOR ONLY A FEW WEEKS IN THE

The Fortunate Woodchuck

Among the few animals that have actually thrived on man's encroaching civilization is the fatted wood-chuck, or ground hog, that unreliable harbinger of spring. Sometimes the woodchuck does awaken from winter hibernation too soon—as early as Ground Hog Day, February 2—but usually it goes right back to sleep, whether it casts a shadow or not. Woodchucks are not very active until March or April, when their tracks in the snow, leading from one hole to another, tell of the search for a mate.

NEWBORN WOODCHUCKS, naked and about four inches long, weigh about an ounce. In two and a half weeks (*below*), fur begins to grow.

NEARLY INDEPENDENT, the sleek youngsters (*below*), at five and a half weeks, are twice as long and six times heavier than at birth.

SPRING. ONE OFTEN PLAYS SENTRY (ABOVE), READY TO WHISTLE AN ALARM

Thirty days later, the breeding den contains from two to seven kits—the single brood of the year—which will grow to be self-sufficient in about eight weeks. Forest-cutting has greatly increased the woodchucks' food supply—clover, alfalfa, beans, fruits and grasses of the open meadows— and consequently they are more numerous than ever. In northern Wisconsin, as many as 30 or 40 per square mile have been counted, their burrows providing handy retreats for many other woodland mammals.

IN A MOCK BATTLE, A FIVE-WEEK-OLD PUP, PUSHED OVER ON ITS BACK, SQUEALS WITH RAGE AND BOWLS OVER ITS ADVERSARY IN TURN.

Opportunist in the Meadow

To the red fox, the opening of the great American forests meant widening opportunities to live and breed—for unlike its deep forest cousin, the gray fox, this is a creature of the open meadowlands. Even its breeding den is usually the remodeled burrow of a woodchuck or other animal in an untilled field. The pups, born between mid-March and mid-April, are weaned at two months but fed and guarded by both parents until they leave the den, almost full-grown, when four months old. Sizable and difficult prey is captured to meet the growing family's needs—including muskrats, skunks, opossums and ground squirrels. Year-round staples, however, are cottontails and meadow mice, whose cycles of abundance and scarcity—10 years and four years respectively—strongly influence the foxes' numbers. Where both are scarce, foxes invade farmyards within their mile or two of hunting territory, a fact which has long since incurred man's enmity but has not affected their numbers. Cunning and swift, they elude guns and traps alike—and in some localities, as here in the western counties of Wisconsin, there are six or more red foxes to a square mile, probably even more than there were before settlement.

BACK FROM THE HUNT, a male red fox carries a ground squirrel to its pups inside the den, whose entrance is visible at left. Unlike other members of the dog family, foxes stalk rather than run down their prey.

THEN, QUICKLY EXHAUSTED, IT FALLS ASLEEP. EVEN BEFORE WEANING, THE PUPS MAY EMERGE FROM THE DEN AT DAWN OR DUSK TO PLAY

6

A World of Grass

I N 1682 La Salle and 22 other Frenchmen floated down the Mississippi River to the Gulf of Mexico, the first men to penetrate the heart of the continent from the north. The nature and dimensions of North America were now becoming known: the Spaniards had settled in Mexico, New Mexico, Arizona and on the California coast; the English were entrenched in the eastern forests; French and English trappers were penetrating Canada through rivers and lakes in their search for beaver pelts. Although La Salle claimed a huge portion of western North America in the name of King Louis XIV, calling it "Louisiana," most of the land between the Mississippi River and the Rocky Mountains was actually unexplored and would stay that way for another hundred years or more. This is because it held little to attract either adventurer or settler. The land west of the Mississippi was merely a featureless sea on which the grasses rippled like waves as far as the horizon. It simply did not hold the promise of wealth; it lacked the gold of Mexico, the timber of the eastern forests or the fur-bearing mammals of the north woods.

The first Europeans to see the grasslands were the members of the Coronado expedition who reached the plains of Quivira (Kansas). They were not impressed. "The country is like a bowl," declared the chronicler of the expedition, "so that when a man sits down, the horizon surrounds him all around at the distance of a musket shot." The expedition found several lakes, but a number of them were salty; there was some tall grass growing near the lakes but "away from them it is very short, a span or less." When exploration finally got under way at the beginning of the 19th Century, these sentiments had not changed. Lewis and Clark endured many hardships in crossing the northern grasslands to reach the Rockies, and spoke disparagingly of them. Zebulon Pike explored the grasslands of Nebraska and Kansas in the fall of 1806 and left with a poor opinion: "a desert—a barrier—placed by Providence to keep the American people from a thin diffusion and ruin." Pike apparently felt that the young United States would do best to settle the bountiful eastern forests rather than try to cross this sea of grass. This desolation impressed other early travelers. Washington Irving considered that the western plain, "vast and trackless as the ocean . . . apparently defies cultivation and the habitation of civilized life." Today, of course, the grasslands are a source of unimagined wealth, the richest agricultural area on the continent. The eastern portion produces the world's highest yields of corn, the central is fruitful with wheat, the western provides grazing for immense herds of cattle.

THE grassland is the most extensive biome in North America, stretching from central Alberta southward 2,400 miles nearly to Mexico City, and from Indiana westward for about a thousand miles to the Rockies. But the grasslands that one glimpses today are markedly different from the sight that greeted the pioneers. Not even the eastern forests have suffered the almost complete destruction that European man has brought to the grasslands. He broke the deep sod and laid bare the bones of the earth to sweeping winds; he poisoned the wolf, the coyote, the prairie dog; he pursued the bison and the pronghorn to the brink of extinction; he shot the eagles from the sky and inadvertently killed the fishes of the rivers with the silt that washed off his farms. Today only remnants of the unbroken sod can be found amidst corn and wheat fields; most of the wildlife species that flourished as recently as a hundred years ago have either retreated into remote areas or cling to survival only in the sanctuaries of parks and refuges. These virgin remnants of the prairie and its surviving animals, combined with the narratives of explorers and travelers, are all that remain to aid us in reconstructing in the imagination what the heartland of the continent must once have been like.

To the pioneers pushing westward out of the eastern forests, the grasslands posed a question—why were there no trees? The answer at first probably appeared simple: there just was not enough rain or it did not fall at the right times of the year to allow trees to grow. It is true that in the western grasslands the rainfall may average only 12 inches a year, much too little for the growth of most trees, and that there is a great variation from year to year in the amount of rain. Making conditions even less hospitable for trees are the high evaporation rate, caused by strong, dry winds, and the baking summer. But this cannot be the whole story, for the eastern portions of the grasslands get up to 40 inches of rain a year, and yet, except along the banks of streams, they have no trees—or did not have them until they were planted as windbreaks by farmers. Clearly something else kept the trees out, and that something was grass. The explanation lies in the characteristics of grass plants themselves. They are uncomplicated mechanisms, efficient at survival and dispersal, and their roots grow at a phenomenal rate. A single rye grass plant, grown experimentally, put out a total of 378 miles of roots in only four months. A grass plant may live for 20 years, its roots interweaving with those of its neighbors. The result is the formation of a thick sod—virtually impenetrable to any seedling attempting to take root. Furthermore, the grasses exhaust the available water near the surface and there is none left over for the seedling.

In the eastern grasslands, where they merged with the forests, the balance between trees and grasses was a precarious one, easily upset. Soil conditions, local topography or winter climate might swing the balance one way or the other. An important factor was the bison, which destroyed many young trees by rubbing against them and prevented the growth of seedlings by trampling them. The greatest influence, however, was fire. During the summer and fall the grasslands are usually dry and as inflammable as tinder. Blazes started accidentally by lightning, or deliberately by Indians to drive game, roared across the grasslands. Grasses are virtually immune to the effects of fire. Though the tops of the plants are burned, their deep roots usually are not seriously harmed; when the rains come again the following spring, they burst out once more in greenery and toss their seeds to the wind. On the other hand, fire is very damaging to the native trees—oaks and hickories—which take several decades to grow again to seed-bearing size, even if their roots escape damage. And by that time there will probably have been other fires.

EARLY travelers were also perplexed by the monotonous flatness of the grasslands, a country smooth as the top of a table, stretching from the Mississippi to the Rockies and broken only by eroded portions known as badlands. The explanation for this flatness lies in the geologic history of the heartland of the continent; for most of the last half billion years, seas have advanced and retreated across it, laying down level beds of limestone, shale and sandstone. Actually, it is not so level as it looks. About 60 million years ago the buckling and uplift of the crust of the earth raised the Rocky Mountains, and as these were attacked and worn down again by the forces of erosion, their debris washed eastward, depositing a smooth layer of sediments out over the plain, thickest near the mountains and becoming thinner to the eastward. Later, there was another episode of mountain building, which raised the present-day Rockies, and a second period of erosion and washing of material to the eastward. The result of this is that the once-flat table is now a gentle 800-mile slope. The western border of Kansas, for example, is about 3,000 feet higher than the eastern border. But so smooth is it, and so slow the gradual ascent of this enormous amount of debris washed down from those ancient mountains, that the traveler feels that the country he is crossing is absolutely flat.

The Rockies influence the grasslands in still another way: they present a high barrier to moist winds sweeping inland from the Pacific. As these winds

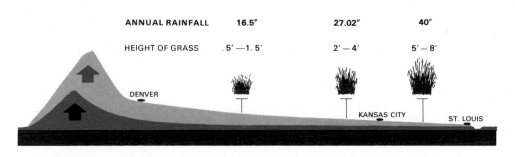

ANNUAL RAINFALL   16.5″   27.02″   40″

HEIGHT OF GRASS   .5′—1.5′   2′—4′   5′—8′

DENVER   KANSAS CITY   ST. LOUIS

THE MID-NATION SLOPE

When two successive upheavals formed the Rocky Mountains, one 60 million (black arrow, left) and the other 15 million (colored arrow) years ago, they disrupted the flat land of the West that had been formed by advancing and retreating inland seas during the Paleozoic and Mesozoic eras (black bar). Silt washed from the new mountains to settle in a gentle slope on the plains all the way to the Mississippi River. Today in the 800 miles from Denver to St. Louis, the land, though appearing level, drops more than four fifths of a mile. Since the mountains take the moisture from the Pacific winds, little rainfall is left for the plains immediately to the east. Consequently, short grasses grow there. But going eastward, vegetation is more lush as rains increase with the moist air carried up from the Gulf of Mexico. Native grasses in Kansas are about 30 inches tall but in Missouri they may grow to eight feet.

119

reach the Rockies, they are forced to rise suddenly; they cool rapidly and the moisture in them condenses, wrung out as rain or snow that falls on the mountains. This creates a "rain shadow" in the lee of the Rockies and accounts for an arid region immediately to the east of them known as the short-grass plains. As the dry winds continue to blow eastward, they slowly accumulate moisture again from the Great Lakes and the Gulf of Mexico, and drop it in a region closer to the Mississippi River, known as the tall-grass prairie. As one travels from the base of the Rockies to the eastern forests, the gradual change in the grasses due to the increasing moisture can be seen clearly. Close to the Rockies the grasses are low-growing and there is much bare soil between their tufts, but in eastern Kansas it grows—or once did—higher than the head of a tall man. The change-over from short to tall grass takes place in central Kansas at about the 98th meridian. This is a kind of dividing line; to the west of it rainfall is usually below 20 inches a year, to the east it is somewhat heavier, usually averaging more than 20 inches annually. And in the neighborhood of the meridian itself is a transition zone of mixed short and tall grasses.

THE grasses have created conditions for animals that are strikingly different from those that exist in forests. A forest-dwelling animal can find shelter from enemies in the maze of trunks, branches, vines and undergrowth—but a grassland animal is exposed. It must either run (like the pronghorn, the bison and the jack rabbit) or it must dig (like the prairie dog and other rodents). On the other hand, open country allows animals to gather in large herds and thus alert one another of the approach of danger. A further difference between the two biomes is in the way the animal inhabitants obtain their food. Much of the vegetation in a forest is high above the ground. To obtain it an animal that lives there should be tall or possess the agility of a squirrel or the wings of a bird. All grassland mammals except the predators can obtain their food simply by bending down to nibble it—another reason large mammals are dominant in the plains. North America cannot match the African plains in the diversity and numbers of its mammalian species, but its grasslands were once a fantastic sight, filled as they were with tremendous herds of bison and pronghorn. There was no part of this immense biome that did not contain one or both of these species, but as a general rule, the pronghorn dominated the drier western and southern portions.

The pronghorn is one of the most truly American of all the animals found on this continent. It evolved on the western plains, along with others of its family, but all save it are now extinct. Furthermore, it has never left North America. It has existed in something closely resembling its present form for more than a million years and is a far more ancient inhabitant than the bison or the elk (which in primeval America was a grassland animal as well as a mountain forest one). Neither the bison nor the elk has gone quite as far as the pronghorn in the development of special adaptations to grassland life. The pronghorn's eyes are unusually large for its head; it has excellent vision for considerable distances and through a wide field. If it detects an enemy it can spurt away at 55 miles an hour, a speed no running animal on the continent can equal. It can sustain a steady pace of nearly 40 miles an hour for almost five miles, and even a 10-day-old pronghorn can outrun most dogs. In part, this ability to run fast and far is due to its extremely large windpipe and lungs, and to its habit of running with its mouth open, thus increasing the intake of air.

The pronghorn's remarkable vision and speed are its main defenses against its ancient enemy, the coyote, and its modern one, man—but not its only defense. It also possesses an efficient signaling system by which it can communicate alarm to other pronghorns, even to ones considerable distances away. While feeding, the herd appears loosely spread out over the grassland, but actually the animals are closely linked by a sentinel system at all times. When one animal becomes alarmed, the muscles under a patch of white hairs on its rump contract and the hairs stand erect—flashing in the sun "like a tin pan," as it has been described by the great naturalist of the North American prairies, Ernest Thompson Seton. Nearby pronghorns are warned and also flash their white patches and begin to run. The signal is thus quickly passed from animal to animal and soon all the scattered pronghorns are fleeing.

These ancient endowments for protection did not, however, prove effective against the modern high-powered rifle. As settlers swept across the grasslands, indiscriminate hunting reduced the pronghorn population from its original estimated 50 to 100 million animals to a mere 19,000 by 1908. Since then, strict hunting regulations and conservation efforts have enabled the pronghorns in the United States to make a phenomenal recovery. There are approximately 350,000 of them today, although undoubtedly we will never again witness the tremendous herds that once raced across the grasslands.

The only other large mammal of the continent whose numbers approached, or possibly surpassed, those of the pronghorn was the bison. Except for its massive strength and herd instinct, the bison does not possess the many physical and behavioral adjustments to the grassland environment that the pronghorn does. It is clumsy and slow-moving; it has relatively poor eyesight and little fear of sound. Although its sense of smell is keen, that sense is useless when it is approached downwind, as both Indians and Europeans discovered. It is also an unusually skittish animal. Coronado's chronicler witnessed the fury of a bison stampede as the animals dashed blindly toward a ravine: "So many of the animals fell into this that they filled it up, and the rest went across on top of them. The men who were chasing them on horseback fell in among the animals, without noticing where they were going. Three of the animals that fell among the cows, all saddled and bridled, were lost sight of completely."

THE bison is the largest land mammal in the New World. The average bull weighs about 1,800 pounds, although some individuals weigh as much as 2,400 pounds. The sheer size of this animal, plus its tremendous numbers, had a great influence on the grasslands; the grass was kept cropped low in the western portion and the growth of trees retarded in the eastern. Trails trampled by the herds were conspicuous features of the landscape and were later used by human migrants across the continent. Although bison were primarily inhabitants of the grassland, they ranged throughout the eastern woodlands also; they were sighted early by English settlers on the Atlantic coast, the first one being reported in 1612 near present-day Washington, D.C.

It is difficult to estimate the number of bison on the continent when European man arrived, but some idea of their profusion can be obtained by a traveler's description in 1834: "The whole plain, as far as the eye could discern, was covered by one enormous mass of buffalo." He stated that a space calculated to be 10 miles by eight miles was so packed with bison that "there was apparently no vista in the incalculable multitude." Most reliable estimates of the primeval population range between 45 and 60 million animals. But by 1810 few remained east of the Mississippi River. The only traces that they left in the

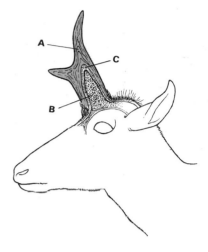

HORNS THAT ARE SHED

The pronghorn has true horns, but they are unique in the animal world because they are branched and are shed annually like antlers. The horn (A, above) is really a sheath growing over a bony core (B) that has a covering of soft hair (C). Unlike antlers, which break off cleanly at the base when shed, the pronghorn is left with the bony core. The hairy covering then hardens, growing in two directions —up to form the horn and down to form the base. About four months after the horns are lost, new ones replace them.

eastern forests were the aforementioned trails their heavy bodies had beaten through the wilderness. As early as 1843 Audubon stated that "there is a perceptible difference in the size of the herds, and before many years the Buffalo, like the Great Auk, will have disappeared; surely this should not be permitted." Despite his warning, the greatest slaughter of any form of wildlife in the world was well under way by the middle of the century.

Millions were slain simply to clear them from land or to prevent damage to railroads; hundreds of thousands perished because carriage robes of bison fur became fashionable; many were killed merely to furnish a meal of bison tongue, the rest of the carcass being left to the scavengers of the plains. The rapidity of the extermination is difficult to envision. It is estimated that 15 million bison still survived by 1865. In that one year alone a million of these were killed, and half of the remainder were gone by 1872. There was probably not a single bison left in the southern portion of the grasslands by 1879. Farther to the north it was more difficult to get at the herds, but the opening of a railroad line in 1880 deprived them of their isolation. Within three years Indian and white buffalo hunters were able to track down the last of the herds in the northern grasslands. The largest herd remaining in the northwest, numbering about 10,000 animals, was methodically eradicated in a few days in 1883 by a simple expedient: sharpshooters were stationed at every water hole where the thirsty animals might attempt to drink.

IN seeking to understand the enormity of this slaughter, it is difficult to accept the various explanations offered at the time—that bison were ruinous to crops, that they spread cattle disease or that they provided meat for Indians and therefore must be eliminated if the Indians themselves were ever going to be subdued. None of these reasons is the whole story, nor could any justify the orgy of butchery that took place. Most of it was sheer senseless waste and is symbolized, not by the tens of millions of animals whose bones were left to bleach on the grasslands, but by a pitiful group of survivors, numbering between 20 and 30 animals, known as the "Lost Park herd" of Colorado. Despite local attempts to protect them, and the knowledge that they constituted possibly a quarter of all the wild bison remaining in the world, this Colorado herd was hunted down by poachers, one by one, until in 1897 the last four—two bulls, one cow and one calf—were slain.

By the beginning of this century, it appeared impossible that the species could survive. Only two wild herds were known to exist on the continent, one in Canada and another numbering 21 animals in Yellowstone National Park. Canada had enacted legislation in the early 1890s that gave the bison the protection of the Northwest Mounted Police; but the penalties for killing bison in Yellowstone were so mild that they barely served as a deterrent to poachers. However, in addition to these two wild herds, a total of 969 animals were owned by individuals and zoos. The largest of these private herds owes its origin to a Pend d'Oreille Indian named Walking Coyote who captured four calves in 1873. By 1884, they had increased to 13 head, which were then sold to a Flathead Indian named Michel Pablo. When the Canadian Government purchased this herd in 1906 to replenish its own stock, it numbered 709 animals. Meanwhile, other efforts were being made to save the species. In 1905 President Theodore Roosevelt established the Wichita Game Preserve in Oklahoma, and it was stocked with 15 bison contributed by the New York Zoological Society. The American Bison Society was formed by conservationists and raised $50,000 to create a National Bison Range in Montana. By 1910, a total of 40 animals had been shipped to the Range, a few of them gifts from individual owners to the people of the United States. Today the remnant herds in the United States have grown to nearly 12,000 animals that find sanctuary on parcels of wild land set aside for them. But before we rejoice at the comeback of the bison, it should be realized that these are all the bison that can ever live in the United States. There simply is not enough land for any more, and in some years as many as a thousand bison must be shot to prevent them from increasing beyond the capacity of the territory to support them.

The bison were the largest and most plentiful of the mammals that competed for forage with the settler's own domesticated cattle. However, other less conspicuous mammals, particularly the jack rabbits and the prairie dogs, also posed an economic threat—and they, too, have been the object of unrelenting persecution. Rabbits and hares of one kind or another live all over the continent, but of them all, jack rabbits are the most characteristic of the prairies and plains. They possess two obvious adaptations for grasslands life—extremely long ears (whence the earlier popular name of jackass rabbit), useful for detecting a predator at a distance, and long hind legs which enable them to run as fast as 45 miles per hour. Because of the jack rabbits' voracious appetite for man's crops, relentless war has been waged against them, and bounties are still offered for their ears throughout their range. Although they are shot, poisoned and driven into nets in cooperative rabbit hunts, they have managed to maintain a tenacious hold on their grassland environment. The settlers were much more successful in killing off the prairie dogs. These rodents not only consume forage needed by livestock but dig up the roots as well. They also make elaborate burrows under the soil; cattle and horses sometimes break their legs by stepping into the holes.

"The prairie dog is, in fact, one of the curiosities of the Far West, about which travellers delight to tell marvellous tales, endowing him at times with something of the politic and social habits of a rational being, and giving him systems of civil government and domestic economy," wrote Washington Irving after his travels on the prairie in 1832. What was a curiosity to the early travelers was a pest to the settlers. In the primeval grassland, a prairie dog "town" sometimes consisted of numerous interconnected communities more than a hundred miles across; one group of towns on the Texas plains was supposed to have covered 25,000 square miles and to have contained about 400 million animals. At the beginning of this century, one authority estimated the number of prairie dogs in Texas alone at 800 million, and he claimed that they consumed more grass than three million head of cattle.

ALTHOUGH there is no doubt that prairie dogs swarmed in the unbroken grasslands, it does not necessarily follow that eradication of every prairie dog in Texas automatically meant forage for three million more cows. For one thing, although they ate a great deal, they also increased the fertility and yield of the grassland. In the same way that earthworms and moles turn over the forest soil, thus enriching it and improving its structure, the prairie dogs were the plows that broke up the compacted sun-baked crust of the prairie. A community of prairie dogs digs as many as 50 holes per acre, each leading to a labyrinth of tunnels that may descend to 14 feet. In the course of these excavations, the animals may dig up about 40 tons of soil per acre, thus enriching it and making it more porous for the growth of the very grasses needed by cattle. It is clear that a somewhat reduced number of prairie dogs would probably have been a beneficial influence in today's grasslands, but their destruction proceeded so rapidly that they are largely extinct throughout their primeval range from southern Saskatchewan to Texas.

As recently as 1963 the U.S. Fish and Wildlife Service spread poisoned grain, as part of its rodent-control activities, on 1,360,200 acres of government and private land in the West and Midwest. Large as this figure may seem, it actually represents a decrease from a decade or so earlier when several million acres were poisoned each year, primarily to kill prairie dogs but also ground squirrels, gophers and other rodents believed to be sufficiently injurious to agriculture to justify poisoning the landscape. These poisons are undoubtedly effective, but they work like a scatter-gun rather than a rifle that pinpoints its target. For one thing, rodents killed by these poisons often die on the surface of the ground, where they are later eaten by predators and scavengers, which in turn are poisoned also. No exact statistics exist on the inadvertent killing of innocent animals in this way, but it is undoubtedly an important factor in the deaths of bears, foxes, eagles, hawks, owls and other animals. One of the rarest of North American mammals, the black-footed ferret, is nearing extinction in the northern grasslands; the primary cause almost certainly is the poisoning campaign directed against prairie dogs, which are the main prey of the ferrets. In addition to secondary poisoning, another effect of these campaigns is that often the poison is eaten by animals for which it was not intended. The kit fox, for example, once occurred throughout the short-grass plains, but it has been nearly exterminated by poisoned bait to kill wolves and coyotes. Another animal that has suffered in this way is the badger, one of the most beneficial of grassland predators. The badger is an expert digger which obtains most of its food by killing pocket gophers, prairie dogs and other rodents in their burrows. But badgers are today much diminished in numbers; they eat the poisoned bait laid out for coyotes, and probably as many badgers are inadvertently killed by the poison as are coyotes.

ALTHOUGH the great poison campaigns are directed primarily at rodents, this does not mean that strenuous efforts have not been made to exterminate predators and, in fact, any animals that appear to dispute modern man's dominance of the grassland. No sooner had cattle and sheep arrived on the prairie than war was declared against the two most efficient predators of the undisturbed grassland community, the wolf and the coyote. Both of these animals had increased in numbers on the abundance of carrion left in the wake of the slaughter of the bison, and the wolf in particular represented a threat to livestock. A sustained effort to eradicate it began in 1914, with the help of Federal funds; in only a decade the wolf was almost completely eliminated within the borders of the United States. An overwhelming number of coyotes has been killed also, but this species has proven much more resilient under persecution than the wolf. Although there is still a bounty on its head in most western states (about 90,000 coyotes a year are killed in federally supported campaigns), the coyote today not only populates many places in the grasslands but it has even extended its range widely. It is possible that the coyote was a primeval inhabitant of the northeastern states, although it was not mentioned by early settlers, who probably mistook it for a wolf. Nevertheless, it is certain that in the present century the coyote has spread from the grasslands as far north as Alaska and east into New England. The first authenticated shooting of one in New York

THE PERILS OF POISON

In his age-old campaign against pestiferous insects, man's principal weapon until recently has been the spreading of poison. The trouble with poison is that all too frequently it also kills other wildlife—a fact which was once catastrophically illustrated by a massive campaign against the Japanese beetle in Illinois. Dieldrin—50 times stronger than DDT —was sprayed over a large beetle-threatened area. Birds bathed in poisoned pools and ate poisoned beetles and worms. Squirrels, rabbits, fish and domestic animals—particularly cats— died by the hundreds. After eight expensive years with even more potent chemicals, and an incalculable loss of wildlife, the tenacious beetle was still unchecked.

State was in 1912, after it had presumably crossed the frozen St. Lawrence River from Ontario. It is now entrenched almost throughout New York State, in nearly every county in Vermont, and even in parts of Connecticut and Massachusetts as well. In addition to this natural spread of the coyote, its numbers and its range in the east have been augmented by escaped or liberated pet animals. In fact, within the past 50 years, coyotes have been seen or killed in every state east of the Mississippi River except Delaware and Rhode Island.

Although the coyote's numbers in the grasslands are today greatly reduced, it has nevertheless been better able to adjust to advancing civilization than any other large predator. This fact is lamented by western stockmen, but not by naturalists. Ernest Thompson Seton wrote: "If ever the day should come when one may camp in the West, and hear not a note of the coyote's joyous stirring evening song, I hope that I shall long before have passed away." Not many frontier expressions have proven to be accurate natural history, but "clever as a coyote" has. A coyote, hunting alone, can catch a pronghorn only when the prey is weakened or unable to flee because of the terrain. But two or more coyotes, using teamwork, can hunt down a healthy pronghorn and do so in open country where the pronghorn has the advantage of speed. A typical maneuver might be for one coyote to separate from its hunting companion, then circle through the brush until it has reached a position on the opposite side of the herd. Then the other coyote springs into the open in such a way that it panics the pronghorn herd into fleeing directly toward its partner. Coyotes also possess extraordinary stamina, as demonstrated by one that was trapped in New Mexico but escaped by dragging away the trap attached to its foot. For 17 days, until it finally succeeded in extricating its paw, it traveled with the trap on its foot, apparently feeding upon birds, sheep and gophers.

The North American birds of the plains and prairies also demonstrate striking adaptations to the grassland environment and the particular way of life it imposes. Since their food is on the ground, there is little reason for grassland birds to fly except to escape an enemy or to migrate. Thus many birds, even though they are able fliers, spend most of their lives on their feet. They are strong walkers and runners, and may cover several miles in a day. A typical example is the California quail, which inhabits arid grasslands. Now reduced in numbers from overshooting, this bird once strutted across the plains in flocks of up to 500. Its tendency to flock, also seen in horned larks, affords the same sort of protection against predators that the herding instinct does for pronghorns. The larks display a further adjustment to the grassland—they do much of their singing while on the wing, there being a dearth of trees to serve as singing posts. The shortage of trees also requires birds to nest on the ground, like prairie chickens, or in underground holes, like burrowing owls.

G ONE, perhaps forever, are the Eskimo curlews—tall, stately birds with long bills that curve downward—which once flew over the grasslands in tremendous numbers. After the decline of the passenger pigeon toward the end of the last century, meat hunters turned to other birds, among them the Eskimo curlew. This bird wintered in the pampas of Argentina, and to get to its nesting grounds in the remoteness of the Canadian tundra, it followed a route that took it over the grasslands from Texas to the prairie provinces of Canada. Its lack of fear and its habit of gathering in large numbers made it particularly easy to kill; curlews were shipped to market by the wagonload and by 1890 had become exceedingly scarce. The last specimen was shot in 1932, although

FIGHTING BUGS WITH BUGS

More effective and infinitely less destructive to the wildlife community than the wholesale use of pesticides is fighting one insect with another. Thus the Japanese beetle was effectively checked in several eastern states when some 34 species of predatory and parasitic insects, all its natural enemies, were imported from the Orient. The female wasp Tiphia vernalis (above) proved deadly effective. This wasp finds a beetle grub and attaches an egg to it; upon hatching, the young wasp devours the grub. Even more efficient is the method of injecting into the soil a type of bacterial disease that attacks beetles but is harmless to worms, plants, other insects, and warm-blooded animals.

there were a number of reliable sightings in the late 1930s. Reports of Eskimo curlews occur to this day, but ornithologists are afraid that these birds may possibly be the nearly identical little curlew of Asia.

No birds of the grasslands better symbolize a way of life in the open than do the grouse. Three kinds of grouse are found in the North American grasslands —the sage grouse, the prairie chicken and the sharptail grouse—and they all put on courtship displays that are among the most spectacular to be seen in any bird species. The sage grouse is the largest North American grouse and it is intimately linked to habitats where sagebrush grows. Its primary food is the buds and leaves of the sagebrush, and it also finds shelter in the plant's tangled growth, its gray plumage almost exactly matching that of the stems and leaves. Before European man reached North America, prairie chickens belonging to several different subspecies were found throughout the grasslands and even inhabited open areas near the North Atlantic coast. The Atlantic form—the heath hen—is forever extinct, and the other subspecies are much reduced both in numbers and in range. The causes for the decline of the surviving subspecies are many. Nevertheless, surely paramount among them are overhunting and habitat destruction. In just one year a century ago, 20,000 greater prairie chickens were sent to market from only a single county in Indiana; today the entire state contains fewer than 6,000 of these birds. In fact, the greater prairie chicken is now rare everywhere south of Canada; even there, it has disappeared from Alberta and is very uncommon in Manitoba and Saskatchewan. The numbers of lesser prairie chickens are even more seriously reduced and almost all of them survive only in Texas; a third subspecies, Attwater's prairie chicken, is virtually extinct and its range is now limited to a small part of southeastern Texas.

ALTHOUGH it may be romantic to urge the preservation of the coyote because of the appeal of its nighttime call, or the restoration of prairie dogs because of their interesting social behavior, these esthetic arguments rarely can resist economic ones. However, in the case of the prairie chickens, there are no economic arguments at all; these birds present no threat to sheepman, cattleman or agriculturist, and one can appeal directly to sentiment and man's innate respect for beauty. If their present decline continues, forever lost will be one of the most stirring sights of the primeval grasslands—the courting dance of the prairie chickens. This dance starts at dawn, with a dozen or more birds sailing out of the sky to alight on a knoll, a dancing platform that has probably been used by generations of its species. Suddenly one male points its head downward, spreads its wings, raises its tail and puffs out its feathers. It then rushes around the platform, stamping its feet so hard that a sound like the beat of a kettledrum comes from the earth. At the same time, two brightly colored air sacs on its neck inflate, and it emits a challenging three-note boom; its tail and wing feathers vibrate rapidly, producing a rustling accompaniment. As soon as one male begins, others join in, stamping, booming and dancing together wildly.

Ernest Thompson Seton, remembering his youth spent in Canada, wrote of the grasslands he knew so well: "Could we but watch it from the moon, the vastness of its loveliness might be fully glimpsed." In not too many years from now, man will have set himself up on the moon and he will be in a position, if he desires, to aim his telescopes at the North American continent. But instead of witnessing the loveliness of the grasslands that Seton knew, he will see a checkerboard landscape of corn and wheat fields, interlaced by muddy rivers and smudged with the shadows of occasional dust storms.

MASTER OF THE GRASSLANDS IN ITS TIME, A DISPLACED ANIMAL TODAY, THE MIGHTY BISON FINDS ITS LAST REFUGE IN PARKS AND ZOOS

Life in the Open

Home for millions of years to a great range of animals, the grasslands now have everywhere been turned to man's uses. Species that once lived here in abundance have been driven away or are so depleted that they are natural curiosities. How they evolved is shown on the next pages in paintings based on the world's richest mammalian fossil beds, while photographs show some survivors.

DURING THE MIDDLE AND LATE EOCENE, 43 to 35 million years ago, western North America looked something like this. Although grasslands had not yet formed, animals were emerging, the descendants of which would become adapted to such an environment. Already two modern orders of hoofed animals had appeared, the odd-toed perissodactyls and the even-toed artiodactyls. Representing the first group are *Orohippus* (13), an ancestral horse; *Hyrachyus* (1), a long-legged rhinoceros; *Helaletes* (14), a primitive tapir; and *Palaeosyops* (15). Representing the artiodactyls are tiny *Homacodon* (7) and *Helohyus* (8), a possible ancestor of the *Suina*, or swine. But of the two groups, only the perissodactyls had begun to evolve teeth for browsing, a first step toward grazing. The two other ungulates in the painting are the ungainly looking *Uintatherium* (2) and *Hyopsodus* (19). These, along with the gnawers *Trogosus* (3) and *Stylinodon* (6), belonged to dying orders.

Among the other animals shown here are such carnivorous mammals as the fox-sized *Sinopa* (10), the saber-toothed *Machaeroides* (12), the stealthy *Patriofelis* (18) and the hyena-like *Mesonyx* (4). All four may have preyed on the primitive rodents *Ischyrotomys* (5) and *Sciuravus* (17), the edentate *Metacheiromys* (9) and the primate *Smilodectes* (16). Also included are *Saniwa* (11), a lizard; *Echmatemys* (21), a turtle; and *Crocodilus* (20), still around today in much the same form.

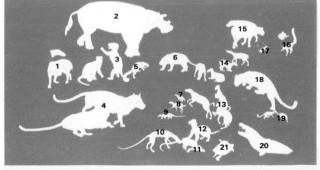

DURING THE OLIGOCENE, between 25 and 35 million years ago, the drying up of the land and the laying down of detritus eroded from the Rockies helped create a savanna-like environment in which the ungulates could come into their own. And for the first time, there was plenty of grass. Although the artiodactyls predominated, the odd-toed perissodactyls made great evolutionary strides. Not only did the first true rhinoceros stock emerge, represented above by *Trigonias* (1) and *Subhyracodon* (22), but *Protapirus* (10), the first true tapir, and *Mesohippus* (3), the first three-toed horse and the first to browse, came into being. On the other hand, *Hyra-*

codon (8), a long-legged rhinoceros, belonged to a dying line.

For sheer bulk, if nothing else, there was *Brontotherium* (9), the largest land mammal ever found in North America. It stood eight feet tall at the shoulder and, with others of its kind, was enjoying a period of maximum development until, with apparent suddenness, it died out.

The predominant artiodactyls showed enormous diversity, but except for the piglike animal *Archaeotherium* (7), and *Aepinacodon* (4), a distant relative of the hippopotamus, they were fairly small, as was *Poëbrotherium* (11), an ancestral camel. Some, like the ruminants *Hypisodus* (12), *Leptomeryx* (17) and

Hypertragulus (18), were not much bigger than the insectivorous *Ictops* (15), the squirrel-like rodent *Ischyromys* (13) or the primitive rabbit *Palaeolagus* (14). *Protoceras* (6), with its bizarre horns, *Perchoerus* (2), the oldest known American peccary, and *Merycoidodon* (21), a plant eater, approached more normal size. The group to which *Merycoidodon* belonged expanded so rapidly in the Oligocene and early Miocene that its fossils outnumber those of all other North American mammals for the period. Among the carnivores depicted are the saber-toothed cat *Hoplophoneus* (16), the foxlike *Hesperocyon* (5), and *Hyaenodon* (19), shown biting down on the lizard *Glyptosaurus* (20).

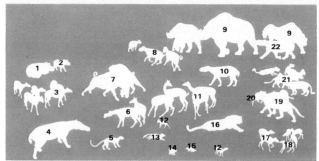

THE EARLY MIOCENE, 25 to 20 million years ago, saw the spread of grass and the rise of animals specialized for life in grasslands. One of the most important developments occurred in the mouth of a descendant of *Mesohippus*. This horse, *Parahippus* (8), had shifted from a browsing dentition to an incipient grazing one, which enabled it to eat grass. A similar trend manifested itself among the artiodactyls; they also had slightly higher crowned teeth, as exemplified in

Merychyus (2), suggesting some ability to graze, while the teeth of a relative, *Promerycochoerus* (5), indicate that it could at least browse. And already *Palaeocastor* (3), a beaverlike rodent, was living a life not unlike that of a prairie dog.

The giants of the period were the perissodactyl *Moropus* (1), a clawed relative of the horse, and the artiodactyl *Daeodon* (10). *Moropus*, confronted here by the dog *Daphoenodon* (4), stood about eight feet tall at the shoulder and dwarfed

another prevalent perissodactyl, the rhinoceros *Diceratherium* (6). *Daeodon*, last and largest of the giant piglike animals, stood six feet tall at the shoulder and was about 11 feet long.

As in the Oligocene, the artiodactyls continued to be more numerous and diversified than the perissodactyls. From camel-llama stock came the small *Stenomylus* (7) and the tall, long-legged *Oxydactylus* (11). And from the *Protoceras* of the previous era came the four-horned, antelopelike *Syndyoceras* (9).

IN THE EARLY PLIOCENE, 12 to nine million years ago, the American grasslands supported a variety of plains animals, including horses of many kinds. Shown here are *Neohipparion* (9), a three-toed horse that failed to survive the drying-out of the area at the end of the Pliocene, and the first of the one-toed horses, *Pliohippus* (10), the descendants of which did survive. The increasingly arid conditions also took their toll among the rhinoceroses, which died out in America by the end of the Pliocene; they are represented by *Teleoceras* (2) and the long-legged *Aphelops* (11).

Among the artiodactyls shown, *Merycodus* (5), one of the pronghorn family, seems a simple creature beside the peculiar *Cranioceras* (3), which did not shed its horns, and *Synthetoceras* (4), which had two pairs of horns—with one set resembling nothing quite so much as a slingshot. Following a trend toward gigantism among the camels, *Megatylopus* (12) stood

15 feet high; it was overshadowed only by *Amebelodon* (1), a shovel-tusked mastodon. *Procamelus* (13) differed from *Megatylopus* in its smaller size. With so many big animals to prey on, including the peccary *Prosthennops* (8), as well as such morsels as the rabbit *Hypolagus* (7) and the horned rodent *Epigaulus* (6), the carnivores flourished. The three here are *Pseudaelurus* (15), a cat, *Hemicyon* (14), a bearlike dog, and *Osteoborus* (16), a hyenalike dog with huge, bone-crushing jaws.

A PRONGHORN BUCK displays its elegant horns, which are usually bigger and more forked than the female's. The prongs help stay an opponent's thrusts in the battles of mating season.

The Pronghorn: Native American

At the end of the Pliocene, when land bridges to Asia and South America rose, many North American animals dispersed to those continents. Llamas wandered south to the Andes, and camels and horses strayed into Asia, there to establish themselves and spread out while their relatives at home, for reasons unknown, eventually dwindled and died out. Of all the larger mammals that had evolved in isolation in North America, only the pronghorn failed to venture beyond the continent. Today, although not nearly as prevalent as it once was, it continues to occupy sections of its ancient range in many western and southwestern states.

Swiftest of the American mammals, the prong-

GALLOPING FROM ALL DIRECTIONS INTO A COMPACT GROUP, STAMPEDING PRONGHORNS TAKE FLIGHT ACROSS THE CHARLES SHELDON REFUGE IN

horn runs easily even over broken ground, bounding on the cartilaginous pads of its feet. Marvelously equipped for speed, it has in addition to its enormous windpipe and lungs a powerful heart twice the size of that of a sheep, an animal comparable in body weight. But capable as it is in fleeing predators and man, the pronghorn suffers from a tragic flaw—curiosity. Nervous, distrustful, timid, it will nevertheless approach almost anything out of the ordinary, as the photographer who took the picture at left discovered. Indians knew this, and often got within shooting range of a pronghorn simply by tying a cloth to a nearby bush and waiting for their inquisitive prey to trot right up and inspect it.

A PRONGHORN FAWN, sensing danger, hugs the ground in an attempt to look inconspicuous. Protectively colored, it lacks the brilliant white rump that sets off the adult of the species.

NEVADA. AS THEY GAIN SPEED, THEY WILL BEGIN TO STRING OUT IN SINGLE FILE, WITH A DOE TAKING THE LEAD, WHILE A BUCK BRINGS UP THE REAR

ALTHOUGH COYOTES WOULD RATHER RUN THAN STAND, THIS ONE SHOWS HOW FIERCE THE SPECIES CAN BE WHEN TRAPPED OR CORNERED

The Persevering Outlaw

As a fur bearer and killer of livestock, the coyote has been trapped, snared, shot, poisoned and even stomped to death (*right*) ever since the West was won. And yet the coyote persists, one of the few animals that seems to be holding its own against man. The reasons why are not difficult to find. It is prolific: seven pups constitute an average litter. It is omnivorous, eating everything from rodents, birds, reptiles, wild game, carrion and an occasional member of its own kind, to acorns, prickly pears, eggs, grasshoppers and other insects. And it is tenacious, with amazing powers of recuperation. Cases of scalped, peg-legged and jawless specimens have been recorded. One healthy coyote when caught had four strands of hog wire fencing buried deep in its flesh; another had its mouth wired almost completely shut and yet had managed to go on feeding.

STOMPING A COYOTE TO DEATH, a trapper assures himself of an undamaged pelt. In the winter, the pelt is at its best—thick and glossy and light in color.

139

A Bird of the Brush

Of all the birds that inhabit the Great Plains, few seem more purely a product of this environment—or more totally adapted to survival in its open spaces—than the sage grouse. Not only does it begin life on the ground, in a shallow nest scraped from the soil by the mother hen, but it spends the greater part of its life earthbound. Camouflaged to blend with the sage bushes among which it dwells, it consumes the buds and leaves of this pungent herb in such quantity that its flesh eventually acquires a strong sage flavor.

For several weeks, between daybreak and sunup during the mating season, the males vie with each other on the so-called arena or booming ground, a well-trod area that may be as long as a half mile and 200 yards wide. Opening and closing their tails, puffing out their chests, they emit booming calls, made possible by an esophagus that can be expanded to 25 times its normal size. Gradually, a hierarchy of males is established, and the male who puts up the strongest showing at strutting and fighting becomes the flockmaster, whose privilege it is to perpetuate the species. The hens come to him one at a time, bypassing the other males, and thus the flockmaster may mate with as many as 80 per cent of the females.

FANNING OUT ITS SPECKLED TAIL FEATHERS, A STRUTTING MALE SAGE GROUSE BEGINS ITS DISPLAY. THE HIGH POINT COMES WHEN IT PUFFS

THE COURTSHIP DISPLAY of a male sage grouse attracts the attention of a much smaller hen. The males may weigh up to eight pounds, making this species the biggest of the American grouse—and one of the larger of the American birds.

OUT A POUCH IN ITS NECK AND EXPOSES THE INFLATABLE SACS, CAUSING ITS HEAD TO ALL BUT DISAPPEAR IN A ROLL OF FLESH AND FEATHERS

Violence from the Sky

The flat Midwest and Great Plains are the spawning grounds of storms, of which one of the smallest, the tornado, is one of the most violent and dangerous. Tornadoes arise here in spring and early summer, born of an unstable weather situation, such as a cold front meeting a warm front. Strong and conflicting winds may combine to form a tremendously powerful mass of whirling air. A tornado's funnel, made up of water droplets mixed with dust and debris, can lift houses, but much of the damage these storms do is a result of abrupt changes of air pressure, great enough to blow up buildings.

THE BIRTH OF A TORNADO is recorded in these photographs. Here, a thunderhead rotates ominously in a counterclockwise direction. The appendage is part of the cloud, not the funnel.

FULLY FORMED, THE FUNNEL SWEEPS TOWARD FARGO, NORTH DAKOTA. THIS STATE AVERAGES THREE TORNADOES ANNUALLY, BUT IN 1957, WHEN

A SHORT WHILE LATER, the tail is almost completely absorbed, and the rotating cloud mass drives forward, spreading darkness as it travels at a speed of about 16 miles an hour.

ONLY 10 SECONDS OLD, the funnel begins to whirl toward the ground. Approaching in its spin a velocity of over 200 miles an hour, it will take less than a half minute to touch down.

THESE PICTURES WERE TAKEN, IT WAS STRUCK BY 13. FROM THE CLOUD SHOWN HERE CAME FIVE FUNNELS, WHICH CAUSED DAMAGE IN THE MILLIONS

7

Mountain Ramparts

OF all the tales told about unknown America, some of the strangest came
from that broken, jagged area now delineated as the western mountains, the
last part of the continental United States to be thoroughly explored. As the
19th Century began, trappers were pushing up the rivers west of the Mississippi
into totally unknown land, and they sent back fantastic stories of mountains
that shone like gold, of weird rock formations, of enormous white bears, of fabu-
lously horned animals that nimbly leaped from crag to crag. These accounts
were dismissed as tall tales by Easterners, but now, of course, we know that
there was considerable truth to most of them.

The opening up of the western wilderness beyond the sea of grass officially
began in 1803. President Thomas Jefferson had just purchased from France
more than a million square miles of land west of the Mississippi, stretching
from New Orleans to the northern Rockies. This, the Louisiana Purchase,
immediately more than doubled the area of the United States. Jefferson was
confident that a useful route could be found across this wilderness to the Pacific
coast, and he organized an expedition, led by his personal secretary, Captain
Meriwether Lewis, and Lieutenant William Clark, both veterans of the early

145

Indian wars. These men were given precise instructions by Jefferson on the route they should follow: first up the Missouri River to its headwaters, then a day's portage over the western mountains to reach the headwaters of the Columbia River, and finally an easy float down the Columbia to the Pacific Ocean.

In May 1804, the expedition set out from St. Louis in three boats. The actual party consisted of 23 soldiers, a slave, two French trappers and the Indian wife of one of the trappers, who served as interpreter. For 15 months they traversed the northern grasslands up the Missouri River, passing through a landscape that the journals of the expedition often noted as "beautiful." But this beauty will never be seen again, for almost the whole of the Missouri River is now a sequence of reservoirs behind high dams, and industries now cluster along its banks. On June 13, 1805, Lewis and a reconnoitering party looked out across a "beautiful plain, where were infinitely more buffaloe than we had ever before seen at a single view." But they also saw rising from the plain "two mountains of a singular appearance and more like ramparts of high fortification than works of nature." Soon they heard the sound of water and saw a cloud of spray rise above the plain like a column of smoke. This was the place that friendly Indians had told them about, and as they approached they heard a roaring "too tremendous to be mistaken for any thing but the great falls of the Missouri . . . the sublime spectacle of this stupendous object which since the creation had been lavishing its magnificence upon the desert, unknown to civilization." The Great Falls, in western Montana, marks the true beginning of the Rocky Mountains; this is the place where the river cascades over a shelf of resistant granite rock to pour at last onto the easily eroded rocks of the plains. And in the distance Lewis and Clark beheld the shining mountains, reflecting not gold but the snowfields that crown their heights.

TODAY the Rocky Mountains rising thus abruptly from the plains are a glorious sight for the traveler, but to Lewis and Clark they indicated only a formidable barrier: "Nothing can be imagined more tremendous than the frowning darkness of these rocks, which project over the river and menace us with destruction." As they ventured into the mountains, fighting off clouds of mosquitoes and midges which bloated their faces, they abandoned their boats and towed canoes against the powerful current. Fear of Indians was now replaced by fear that they would find no Indians to aid their passage. For a month they wandered, skirting avalanches, cutting through ravines, seeking out passes, until they eventually surmounted the Continental Divide. And, in mid-August 1805, an Indian gave them salmon from a creek, evidence that here was western water—water that flowed toward the Pacific Ocean. But their journey through the mountains still was not over; they had to negotiate further ranges and endure penetrating cold and short rations before they finally reached the mouth of the Columbia River. "Not any of us have yet forgotten our sufferings in these mountains," wrote Lewis, "and I think it probable we never shall."

The expedition returned to St. Louis in September 1806, backtracking eastward from the Pacific over much the same route, although several new passes were attempted. The men now knew that Jefferson had been dead wrong about the western mountains. There was no river link between the Atlantic and Pacific—the streams were too swift, shallow and choked with fallen trees and boulders. But Lewis and Clark had proved that beyond the sea of grass lay a world of giant peaks where game was plentiful, timber tall and furs bountiful.

Now that the western portion of the continent has been explored thoroughly,

BUILT FOR FAST WATER

In many swift mountain streams, currents are strong enough to sweep fish away from their foraging grounds near the river bed. These two different species of the Colorado River, the rare Gila cypha (above) and the more common humpback sucker (below), have the same enlarged-back adaptation that helps them stay near the bottom. When the swift water strikes the forward edge of these backs, the deflected force tends to push the fish downward. In this way, both the two-foot-long sucker and the Gila, which is half as large, are aided by the currents in keeping in place while the flowing waters bring them a constant supply of food.

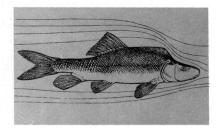

we can understand the complex of ranges, valleys and isolated summits that so bewildered Lewis and Clark. Basically, the western mountains consist of three long chains that extend north-south and nearly parallel each other—the Rockies, the Sierra Nevada-Cascades and the Coast Ranges. All three of these chains are different, both in appearance and in geologic history, from the Appalachians of the eastern part of the continent. The western mountains look different because of their sawtooth profiles, deep gorges and precipitous cliffs. These peaks are earmarks of geologic youthfulness, for the western mountains came into existence no more than some tens of millions of years ago, and indeed several of them may still be rising. The mountains of the east once were jagged also, but that was about 250 million years ago. Today they have the rounded contours of an ancient chain; what remains of some of them are only the worn-down stumps of once much higher mountains. Almost all of the eastern peaks, except Mount Washington in New Hampshire and Mount Katahdin in Maine, are clothed with trees or shrubs to their very summits. By contrast, the upper portions of numerous western peaks, because of their great height, are bare of trees and often of any plant growth at all.

THE longest and most easterly of the three great western mountain chains is the Rocky Mountain system, which extends from the Brooks Range of northern Alaska southward to central New Mexico. Under the single name Rockies, we lump together a complex of many small ranges, such as the Bitterroots between Idaho and Montana, the Big Horns of Montana and Wyoming, the Tetons of Wyoming, the Front Range of Wyoming and Colorado, and the Sangre de Cristo of Colorado and New Mexico. Each of these lesser ranges possesses its own individuality and its own splendors; as each was in turn explored, its beauties were declared to surpass the previously discovered ones. In 1806 Zebulon Pike first saw the mountain peak in Colorado later to be named for him and compared it to "a small blue cloud." He tried to climb it but failed. Captain John C. Frémont did succeed in reaching the summit of the peak that now bears his name in the Wind River Mountains of Wyoming and said of it that "Nature had collected all her beauties together in one chosen place."

The second western chain is the Sierra Nevada-Cascades complex, which extends from the Kamloops of British Columbia to southern California. The northern part, the Cascades, contains perhaps the most majestic string of peaks on the continent, including the picturesque volcanic cones of Rainier, Hood, Adams, Jefferson and others. Near Mount Shasta in northern California, the Cascades merge with the Sierra Nevada part of the range. To one early fur trader struggling across it, the Sierra represented "a defiant wall of rock." Although the shortest of the three western chains, the Sierra-Cascades contain some of the least spoiled wilderness, the highest North American mountains south of Canada, the only groves of giant sequoia in the world, the glacier-carved Yosemite Valley and the volcano-created Crater Lake.

Finally, rimming the western borders of the continent, and in places rising directly out of the Pacific Ocean, are the Coast Ranges. These were probably the first of the western mountains to be seen by European man; as early as 1542, Juan Rodriguez Cabrillo, cruising the coastline, said of them: ". . . sailing along close to land, it appears as though they would fall on the ships."

These were the three chains that the Lewis and Clark Expedition crossed. As they left the plains and began the ascent into the first of them, the Rockies, they began to encounter a different kind of wildlife than the bison and prong-

DEATH OF A RIVER

These three vignettes show what happens to a stream when raw sewage, one of the most common pollutants, is dumped into it. In the first drawing, fish, shrimps, insects and snails of many species swim in

clear, richly oxygenated water above a clean gravel bed in which aquatic plants grow. As the stream is polluted, decomposing bacteria multiply in great quantities, feeding off the sewage and consuming the dissolved oxygen in the water.

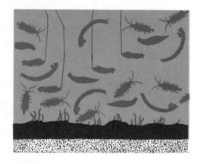

The original plant and animal population is killed off and replaced (middle) by a dense population of rat-tailed maggots, whose air tubes get oxygen from the surface, sludge worms, blood worms, mosquito wrigglers and leeches. Black,

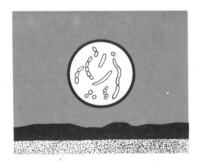

gelatinous algae cover the bottom, adding to the foul odor of decomposition. In the last picture, all oxygen has been consumed as indicated by the gray shading; noxious gases bubble to the surface and only nonoxygen breathing bacteria survive.

horn they had been seeing ever since they departed from St. Louis. They floundered through unimaginable beaver ponds, and at the Great Falls of the Missouri River, they caught their first western trout, a sure indication that they were leaving the grasslands. North American trout—which include some of the fishes we call "trout" as well as some we call salmon—tens of thousands of years ago were divided into two groups separated by the flooded Mississippi valley. To the east, there evolved the Atlantic salmon, as well as brook trout and lake trout, both of which, properly speaking, are not true trout but are related to the European charrs. To the west, in primeval America, were found the rainbow and cutthroat trout. But man has changed this distribution pattern markedly by stocking rainbow trout all over the continent and by importing the European brown trout into American waters because it is more tolerant of pollution. The trout caught by Lewis and Clark at the Great Falls were known as cutthroat because their gleaming bodies are slashed with red lines under the chin. The cutthroat was probably the original trout that invaded from Asia and was the ancestor of the rainbow; in aboriginal America it had a wider distribution than the rainbow, living in mountain lakes and rivers from Alaska to California and throughout much of the Rockies. There were once almost as many races of cutthroats as there were rivers, but overfishing, pollution and introduction of other fishes have reduced them to perhaps half a dozen types. Rainbow trout, more aggressive than the cutthroat, have been transplanted into cutthroat waters, with the result that the cutthroat survives only in headwater streams.

A further indication that Lewis and Clark were leaving the plains and ascending the mountains was the increasing presence of the grizzly. The Plains Indians warned the Americans about this huge beast, but the members of the expedition were skeptical about its reputed size and ferocity. They had already become acquainted with the black bear, which ranged throughout almost all of forested North America, and had found it an inoffensive animal easily killed with a well-placed shot. They soon changed their opinion about the grizzly. Lewis wrote after one of the early encounters: "The wonderful power of life which these animals possess renders them dreadful . . . we had rather encounter two Indians than meet a single brown bear."

THE group of animals classified as bears belongs primarily to the Eurasian and North American continents, with only three exceptions: the spectacled bear of the South American Andes, the sun bear of southeast Asia and the sloth bear of India. The bears evolved comparatively recently, during the middle Miocene, and may have shared a common ancestry with dogs. About 18 million years ago some of these ancestors began to change markedly: their skulls became massive, their teeth blunt and heavy, their legs stocky, their tails reduced to mere stubs. These changes in structure went hand in hand with changes in habit. They substituted power for speed; they no longer pursued prey, like fleet dogs, and their grinding teeth afforded them a diet of plant food as well as meat. Unlike most mammals, which walk on their toes, bears travel on the soles of their feet like men. Like men also, they can rotate their forearms, which accounts for their skill in seizing prey, digging up roots and even climbing.

Aside from the polar bears of the Arctic, North America is inhabited by two groups of bears—the black bears and the brown bears. But color is an unreliable guide to the two species. "Black" bears may range in color from black to cinnamon, and both of these extremes may occur even in the same litter; "brown" bears may range from pale gold to dark brown or even almost black. The grizzly is the most famous of the North American brown bears, and at one time it was the most abundant, ranging throughout much of the western third of the continent from Alaska to northern Mexico. Its common name of grizzly was derived from the scattered white hairs on its back which give it a grizzled appearance. Some of the light-colored grizzlies appeared almost white when the sun shone on them, and Lewis and Clark often referred to them as "white bears." The grizzly is set apart from other bears not only by its light-colored shaggy coat but by its high shoulder hump, formed by a mass of powerful muscles that drive the front legs. Its head is massive, its ears small and its forehead high—all of which combine to give its face a concave, or "dished," profile. Its front claws are very long and almost uncurved, in contrast to the short, curved claws of the black bear, making it a somewhat less agile climber.

THE grizzly was given the scientific name *Ursus horribilis*—"the horrible bear"—in 1815 by a taxonomist who had never seen one and who relied largely on evidence from another man who had never seen one either, yet declared boldly that "He is the enemy of man and literally thirsts for human blood." This was a grossly inaccurate statement. Except for the skunk, the grizzly is indeed the master of all other mammals on the continent: mountain lions, wolves and black bears retreat at its approach, even abandoning their kills to it. But as far as man is concerned, grizzlies have been no more prone to unwarranted attack than the black bears. Characteristically, the first grizzlies seen by Lewis and Clark fled, although later Lewis reported that they "have now become exceedingly troublesome; they constantly infest our camp during the night." Infesting a camp in search of food is different from attacking. An unprovoked grizzly is not dangerous, although in justice to the people who annihilated this animal because they were convinced of its ferocity, it did not take much to provoke one. A female with cubs was easily angered; a wounded or surprised grizzly could be fierce.

Although black bears still inhabit much of their former range, and in fact are numerous in many mountainous areas of the eastern states, the grizzly has been virtually extinguished south of the Canadian border. Its decline began with the flood of humans through the western mountains on the way to the California gold fields. To the miners, the presence of such a large carnivore was a source of fear, and also of meat and sport. Cattlemen later joined in the slaughter, for some bears had taken to preying upon livestock. Today only about a thousand grizzlies survive in the United States, exclusive of Alaska, and they are all in isolated portions of the northern Rockies. Each one killed pushes the species a little closer to extinction, for the grizzly's breeding potential is extremely low. Since grizzlies do not mate until they are four or five years of age, and since a female gives birth to a litter usually of two cubs only every second or third year, they are slow to replenish animals killed.

In a few years, probably the only grizzlies left alive on the continent, outside of Alaska and Canada, will be the approximately 200 that inhabit Yellowstone National Park—"that last blessed haven of the fugitive from inevitable and nearly universal destruction," as Ernest Thompson Seton described it. Yellowstone is both one of the wonders of the continent and a landmark in the history of modern man's sudden awakening to the necessity for wildlife conservation. Lewis and Clark passed just to the north of Yellowstone and never saw it. Indians had warned them away from this "region possessed of spirits which no man could approach." Today we know the spirits were geysers, mudpots, mammoth springs, glass mountains and petrified wood, all of which must have seemed manifestations of the supernatural to the Indians. Yellowstone was discovered in 1807 by John Colter, a member of the first Lewis and Clark expedition who later went there on his own. He met Captain Clark in St. Louis several years afterward and told him of the place. Clark duly noted "boiling spring" and "hot spring brimstone" on the official Lewis and Clark Expedition map, but Colter's descriptions of the other wonders seemed too fanciful to be true, and they do not appear on the map.

In the next half century other men explored Yellowstone and confirmed that Colter had not been spinning tall tales. In 1872 an act of Congress placed Yellowstone under federal protection "for the benefit and enjoyment of the people." For the first time in modern man's sorry chronicle of mindless use of natural resources, wild land had been set aside for the future under national protection. The establishment of Yellowstone was not universally regarded as a wise step at the time, and Congress wavered on the advisability of maintaining it; members declared that the federal Government was not supposed to go into "show business," nor should it "engage in raising wild animals." Nevertheless, the idea of national parks was infectious, and by 1916 Congress had authorized 49 of them, mostly in the western mountains. From this nucleus have grown today's 108 national parks and monuments, representing 13 million acres in which the land and wildlife of primeval America are forever inviolate. This total was swelled by 9.2 million acres, with the possibility of 50 million more within 10 years, in 1964 when the Wilderness Bill was finally passed after a decade of struggle by conservationists to ensure that other wild areas that formerly were part of national forests and refuges be afforded the additional—and permanent—security of perpetual preservation.

The "blessed haven" of Yellowstone has offered sanctuary not only to grizzlies but to other animals swept aside before the human tide advancing upon the West—to moose, to the well-known elk herd that migrates between Yellowstone and the refuge at Jackson Hole, and to the trumpeter swan. Once found throughout the central and northern portions of the continent, this swan was pushed farther and farther north by ceaseless shooting and draining of its breeding marshes and lakes. The largest of all North American waterfowl, its size and its resounding trumpeting call made it a conspicuous target. Thirty years ago, it was very nearly extinct: its total numbers were estimated to be about 500 birds in British Columbia and 73 in the United States, all in Yellowstone and a nearby national wildlife refuge. But the conservation conscience of the nation had been awakened, as was typified by an incident in 1941 when a proposed army artillery range endangered a population of swans. President Franklin Roosevelt dashed off a memo to the Secretary of War: "The verdict is for the Trumpeter Swan and against the Army. The Army must find a different nesting place!" Since then protection against shooting has enabled the swan to make the long flight back from the edge of extinction. There are about 600 trumpeters in the United States today.

As Lewis and Clark crossed the high plains, headed for the Rockies, they often remarked on the great numbers of elk they saw, and the meat of these animals soon became a prime source of food during their wanderings through the mountains. In primeval America, the elk was a widely distributed member of the deer family, ranging from the Pacific Ocean very nearly to the Atlantic, from the Northwest Territories of Canada almost to the Mexican border. Actually "elk" is a misnomer. This animal is closely related to the red deer of Europe, but for some unknown reason the early settlers who encountered it in the East gave it the name that more properly belongs to the European form of what we call "moose." This confusion has continued to the present day, but it has been somewhat alleviated by calling the American form "wapiti," the name used by Algonquian Indian tribes. When the white man arrived, there were six forms of wapiti in North America, but the eastern one was killed off so promptly that only a single museum skin and a few skulls survive to mark the fact that it ever lived at all. The Merriam elk of the mountains of Arizona and New Mexico is also extinct, and the Tule, or "dwarf," elk of California nearly so. The Manitoba elk of the Canadian provinces of Manitoba and Saskatchewan, and the Roosevelt elk, now restricted largely to the Olympic Mountains of Washington, are both at low population levels. The only race that survives in respectable numbers is the Rocky Mountain elk; practically the entire North American population of some 350,000 animals lives in the United States Rockies, although there are some in Canada and Alaska. This race has also been used to restock ranges formerly occupied by extinct races in areas such as Michigan, New Mexico and Virginia. However, the threat of further persecution still hangs over the Rocky Mountain herds. They are becoming so abundant in some places that they compete for forage with man's own livestock; if they continue to increase, there will no doubt once again be heard a plea by ranchers to wipe them from the landscape.

HIGHER yet in the mountains, Lewis and Clark encountered two animals typical of the western peaks, the wild goat and sheep. The Rocky Mountain goat—actually not a goat at all, but a goat antelope related to the European chamois of the Alps—can clamber over the high rocks with such uncanny skill that it eludes most predators. The bighorn sheep bounding among the mountain crags also seemed immune to killing by man, and Lewis wrote: "These inaccessible spots secure them from all their enemies, and the only danger is in wandering among these precipices, where we should suppose it scarcely possible for any animal to stand." It might have seemed that these animals would be safe from man, but this did not prove true. Bighorn sheep probably were originally extremely plentiful, and in 1800 there were an estimated two million of them in the mountains of the United States. Only about 160 years later, this number was reduced to scarcely more than 7,700 animals. There is no single cause for this precipitous decline. Wagon trains traversing the mountains found the sheep an easy source of provisions, and no doubt deep inroads were made into their populations. However, the bighorns continued to decline even after shooting lessened. The probable reason is that the remaining sheep were crowded into small areas where they had to compete for forage with other wild grazing animals, such as elk that had similarly retreated into the mountains, as well as with man's own domesticated sheep. These European sheep brought with them disease organisms which the wild ones had never encountered; the European sheep had had thousands of years in which to develop resistance to the organisms, but the bighorns sickened rapidly and, because they were living under crowded conditions, infections spread rapidly. Even so, epidemics would not have been unduly severe had predators, such as wolves and mountain lions, been abundant enough to destroy the infected animals before they could spread disease further. But there were few predators: the sheepmen had declared relentless war on them.

The wapiti, the grizzly and the bighorn are conspicuous mountain mammals, but others—burrowers like the pika, marmot and northern pocket gopher—are

A MOUNTAIN BIRTH

When a bighorn sheep ewe is about to give birth, she leaves the band for a secluded narrow ledge. There the newborn lamb (above) has barely enough room to huddle or stand under the mother's body and nurse. But in this dizzy spot, the ewe is well placed to protect her offspring from enemies, particularly the golden eagle, which is always on the lookout for young to carry off. As it starts to move about, the lamb must curb its natural friskiness in order to negotiate the narrow ledge. But after only a week of this hazardous ledge-life, it is well accustomed to heights and so agile and strong that already it can keep up with short movements of the band.

more rarely seen. The pika, in size and appearance reminiscent of a guinea pig, fills a specialized niche, living only in avalanche areas at or above timber line between Mount McKinley, Alaska, and northern New Mexico. Its furred feet with their hairy soles give it excellent traction as it progresses from rock to rock. But its behavioral adaptation of cutting grass and other plants for winter fodder is what permits its survival in this specialized habitat. Seen from a distance, the boulders of a landslide appear to offer little opportunity for life. However, soil has collected among the jumbled rocks, and clumps of grass, herbs and even shrubs have gained rootholds. During the brief summer growing season on the mountain heights, the meadows above timber line break out in greenery. That is when the pika harvests enough plant materials to last throughout the long winter. This little haymaker of the rockslides works busily, cutting off stems and branches close to the ground, then scooping them into bundles almost as large as itself and carrying them to rocks that are bathed in sunshine. There the fodder is piled into miniature haystacks and allowed to cure slowly, small amounts of cuttings being added to each pile daily, with the result that they do not become moldy.

Sharing much the same sort of high-altitude habitat as the pika are two kinds of marmots, the hoary and the yellow-bellied, both related to the familiar woodchuck of the lowland clearings. The hoary marmot usually lives about timber line, either in rocks or in mountain meadows. But the smaller yellow-bellied, which also lives lower down, almost always locates its burrow in the rocks. Unlike the pika, which is active throughout the winter, the marmots hibernate. A third way of life in the high western mountains is demonstrated by the northern pocket gopher, which ranges from southwestern Canada to the mountains of northern New Mexico. Various kinds of pocket gophers live at elevations from sea level to mountain slopes, but this one is almost always found above 8,000 feet. It does not hibernate like the marmot, nor does it spend the summer aboveground storing caches of hay like the pika. Rather, it passes almost its entire life underground, digging through the soil of high mountain meadows in search of bulbs and roots. If a gopher were the size of a man, and its excavation rate were stepped up proportionately, it has been calculated that it would be able to dig a tunnel nearly half a yard in diameter and seven miles long during one 10-hour day. Appropriately enough, the name "gopher" is derived from a French word for "honeycomb."

THE Sierra Nevada-Cascade system has suffered less despoilment than the Rockies, in part because of its inaccessibility, in part because by the time it was invaded by man, America had awakened to the irreparable losses of wilderness it had suffered. On June 25, 1864, President Lincoln signed a bill granting the state of California a tract of land that includes Yosemite and the Mariposa grove of sequoias. The federal Government had often granted land to states before, but this bill was out of the ordinary. The grant was made "upon the express conditions that the premises shall be held for public use, resort and recreation and shall be held inalienable for all times." John Muir arrived in California only a few years after that. His impassioned writings made the beauty of the Sierras known to many people, among them Ralph Waldo Emerson, whom he invited to cross the continent and join him "in a month's worship with Nature in the high temples of the great Sierra Crown." The aging Emerson accepted, and in 1871 noted in his journal the "grandeur of these mountains perhaps unmatched in the globe." Muir was tireless in his fight for conservation in the

West; six superb national parks—Sequoia and Yosemite in the Sierras, Mount Rainier and Crater Lake in the Cascades, Glacier and Mesa Verde in the Rockies —owe their establishment in large part to him.

Perhaps the most abundant, and certainly the most appealing, of the small mammals of these California mountains is the Sierra chickaree, or red squirrel. It is a strikingly handsome animal, its dark-brown back tinged with red, its dark tail glinting with silver. It is restless, noisy and graceful, chattering loudly as it works through the high branches of the forest, gathering enormous numbers of seeds for winter food. Whole cones are cached in small piles in the earth; a single chickaree was found to have stowed away about 500 of them in an area of only 50 feet square. John Muir estimated that possibly more than half of all the cones of Sierra evergreens pass through this squirrel's paws to be stored—and for sequoia cones that figure might be as high as 90 per cent. This is extremely helpful to forestry workers, who cannot harvest sequoia cones themselves because they grow so high up: they rob the chickaree's stores for seed cones. Thus the chickaree serves as a gardener in the Sierras, accounting for the planting of a large proportion of the trees that take root.

ONLY a few explorers passing over the Sierras ever saw a giant sequoia before a hunter chanced upon the huge trunks of the North Calaveras Grove in 1852. Shortly thereafter, two promoters stripped the bark from one of these trees to a height of 116 feet and shipped it for exhibition in the eastern cities and eventually in the Crystal Palace in London. The London exhibit was a failure, since no one would believe that the immense stretch of bark came from a single tree. The desecration of this sequoia resulted in an outcry in the United States, and James Russell Lowell even suggested the establishment of a society for the prevention of cruelty to trees. *Harper's Weekly* later reported that the monarch sequoia, stripped of its protective cover of bark, was decaying, having been peeled "with as much neatness and industry as a troupe of jackals would display in clearing the bones of a dead lion." But this assault was only the beginning: whole sequoia groves were soon under attack by ax, saw and dynamite as lumbermen began to calculate the wealth that the timber in a single trunk would bring. But the venture failed because of the fortunate circumstance that the wood of the sequoia proved to be brittle; it shattered as the giant trees fell to earth, even those that landed on specially prepared beds of brush. However, the attack upon the groves was ruthless and rapid, and a great many trees were felled before the folly was realized. Now national parks and forests are attempting to preserve them in perpetuity, and also the wildlife communities they shelter: among birds, for example, Stellar jays, white-headed woodpeckers and Sierra grouse, as well as chickarees and other creatures.

Of the three mountain ribbons that stretch through the western portion of the continent, the most intruded upon has been the Coast Ranges, except for inaccessible portions along the inland passage to Alaska and remnants preserved in state and national parks. The reason is that they could be approached directly from the coast, whereas one had to make difficult trips across grasslands or deserts to reach the Rockies or Sierras. The jewel of the coastal chain is the small range known as the Olympic Mountains near Seattle. Much of the Pacific Northwest was being heavily exploited during the last century, but the Olympic Peninsula remained virtually unknown. Its isolation, its steep mountains, its dense rain forest, all delayed serious intrusions by man until it was established as a national park. Unfortunately the national park came a little too late to save the magnificent Olympic wolf, which was poisoned and hunted, probably to extinction. But here the rare Roosevelt elk have found sanctuary; mountain goats transplanted from British Columbia and Alaska have also thrived and multiplied.

Symbolic of the lost wilderness of the Coast Ranges south of the Olympics is the California condor, a black-and-white vulture with a wing span that often exceeds nine feet. Unlike the great auk, Carolina parakeet, passenger pigeon and other birds whose decline is attributable directly to the white man, the condor was already a rare bird before Europeans arrived in North America. It is an ungainly and ill-equipped survivor of the Pleistocene. During the ice ages, these gigantic vultures thrived on the abundant carcasses of mammoths and other large mammals; when these animals became extinct several thousand years ago, there was still enough carrion in primeval America for them to exist in reduced numbers. Lewis and Clark saw a condor at the mouth of the Columbia River in 1806, but such sightings probably represented the northern limit of the condor's range; these birds at that time lived chiefly in the coastal mountains of California. The arrival of modern man in these mountains meant also the arrival of new hazards for the condors—wanton shooting, stealing of eggs by collectors, poisoned carcasses put out by ranchers to kill carnivores, destruction of habitat by fire, disturbance of these shy birds by photographers and by the building of roads and trails. Their natural and gradual decline turned into a rout. They were virtually extinct in Washington and Oregon by 1850, although a few birds may have been seen there as recently as 1904; the small numbers that inhabited Baja California disappeared by about 1930. By 1950, condors bred mainly in two small mountainous areas of the Los Padres National Forest in southern California, and their total population was estimated to be about 60 birds.

ALTHOUGH their breeding grounds were set aside as sanctuaries in 1951, the condors have not made the anticipated comeback. On the contrary, their numbers have dwindled; today there may be only 40 or so birds alive. Several factors have caused the decline. Several condors are known to have been shot in recent years, and there probably have been other unrecorded deaths by gunning. At least two birds were killed in one year when they fed on ground squirrels that had been poisoned as part of a federal rodent-control program. Finally, intrusion of people near the sanctuaries set aside for them has caused birds to desert their nests. In a species with a large population, these factors would be inconsequential. But the condor is in peril of immediate extinction, and each bird lost represents a loosening of the species' foothold on survival.

A last-ditch attempt is now being made by the National Audubon Society, the state of California and local conservation groups to halt shooting and to patrol the sanctuaries so that the birds may be undisturbed. Yet, the condor is probably doomed, and with it will go a sight as spectacular as the geysers of Yellowstone or the sequoias of the Sierras—these magnificent aerialists soaring effortlessly over the crests of ridges like some prehistoric birds. Perhaps the fate of the condor was sealed when the mammoths, sloths, dire wolves and other ice-age animals went into extinction, but its decline could have been a gradual one. And although this can be blamed on the rigors of natural selection, man must take the responsibility for its sudden decline. No one knows for sure how soon the last condor will disappear from the skies, but when it does, much of the soaring freedom of the primeval landscape will have departed with it.

SNUG IN ITS CANYON NEST, A TRADE RAT SLEEPS AMONG CLUTTER FROM A RANCH WHERE IT HAS TRADED CONES FOR BUTTONS AND STRING

The High Country

From the Kansas border to the Front Range of Colorado, the land gradually inclines for some 300 miles to a level of about 6,000 feet, where prairies are overshadowed by peaks 14,000 feet high. Here, crowded together within a mere mile and a half, are many different worlds of nature, linked by transients like the canyon-dwelling golden eagle, hunter of the grassland domain of badger and kit fox.

BATTLING A BROWN RAT, the prairie rattlesnake strikes. Its fangs must be deeply imbedded to make the poison effective.

STRIKING BACK, the rat, still vicious though it has been struck 12 times, seizes the snake's lower jaw and tries to make a kill.

SHRIEKING IN ANGER, the rat rolls over, kicking convulsively while the wounded rattler retracts, its jaws open wide (*above*).

A Predator's Fight for Life

In the high country where the prairies meet the mountains, death strikes swiftly for many small animals, as the dominant predators—some of them among the largest of North American carnivores— seek out their prey. Sometimes, however, as the pictures show, the victim will turn unexpectedly to rend his enemy. The prairie rattlesnake, one of the 30-odd North American species, does not normally experience much opposition from the rodents and rabbits which it consumes: its venom, a primarily hemotoxic poison which destroys the victim's blood

cells, is sure death to its small prey. In the controlled experiment photographed here, however, the rattler, released near the nest and young of a female brown rat, had literally to fight for its life. The blood-cell-dissolving poison which it repeatedly injected into the rat works much more slowly than the nerve-paralyzing agents of a coral snake, cobra or some of the South American rattlesnake species, and furthermore, the prairie rattler, which averages four feet in length, is also one of the smaller and less toxic of the big rattlesnake family. Thus the encounter

By this time, the snake is striking in self-defense, its venom production unable to keep up with the repeated injections. It was an hour before the rat lay dead (*below*), and the snake, too badly injured to swallow its prey, at last crawled away.

was not quite as one-sided as it might at first seem. But like all vipers, the prairie rattler has been feared and hated by man ever since the first pioneers and settlers began to open up these western lands. Although snake bite accidents were and still are rare here—it should be remembered that the rattler would rather flee than fight if it has any choice in an encounter with man—thousands were killed as the tide of settlement flowed over the land. Today, though they are still prevalent in cattle country, the number of rattlers has been considerably reduced.

JUST OUT OF THE NEST, the early bird—a young American magpie—swallows a worm which it has found on open prairie. Here its showy white markings make it easy prey for a falcon.

From Worm to Falcon

One of the most universal and basic food animals is the earthworm. On the high, dry prairies and foothills of Colorado, the earthworm is eaten both by small predators like the red ants and large ones like the magpie. How far-flung the web of predation that begins with a worm may be is shown in three examples here and on the following pages. In this case, the ultimate predator is the prairie falcon (*opposite*), which courses low and often strikes its prey on the ground. Magpies and other birds of the open country are its chief prey except in the late spring, when it feeds its newly hatched young on ground squirrels and other rodents, which are vulnerable because they, too, are busy providing for families.

PREY FOR THE FALCON, the magpie is plucked and eaten where it was caught. In a predatory turnabout, the falcon's eggs could also furnish a meal for a magpie.

158

A CLASSIC SPRING FOOD CHAIN here begins at night when a ground beetle seizes an earthworm in its powerful mandibles, tearing it into pieces. The next morning, a Colorado chip- munk discovers the beetle under a stone. Picking it up, the chipmunk gets its nose skinned by the beetle's mandibles, but eats the insect anyway, thus varying the diet of seeds and ber-

IN ANOTHER CHAIN of events, an army of red ants overcomes a large worm by injecting it with formic acid. The paralyzed and bloated victim is carried away to the anthill (above) for all to eat—but the foraging ant armies are attacked in turn by a spiny lizard. Unaffected by the acid and their swarming counterattack, it consumes dozens. The lizard lives among

A Web of Food Chains

On the Colorado prairies, parched by droughts, spring is a welcome season. Then rain pours down, often for a week or two, and mountain freshets roar over dry creek beds to the grasslands below. As the water table rises, worms come to the surface and on the first sunny days are eaten by many animals, like beetles and ants, that do not dig for them. Other predators are out, too, looking for the worm feeders or for those that feed on them. The niches which these creatures occupy, their diurnal or nocturnal activities and their adaptations determine when, how and by what predator they may be caught. Thus food chains are spun, in an elaborate web, depending on the season and the animals' habits. Here between plain and mountain, food chains also vary with altitude—some prairie dwellers, such as the chipmunk, the lizard and the snake shown at left, range right up through 8,000-foot Rocky Mountain canyons where golden eagles and pumas live.

ries normal for this season. At sundown the chipmunk, going home to sleep in a rock crevice, is stalked and killed by a kit fox, a carnivore that has just embarked on its nocturnal hunt.

rocks near water and so becomes vulnerable to a garter snake, which lurks there looking for cold-blooded prey. The garter snake, last of the snakes to hibernate in the fall and the first

one to appear in the spring, is then itself caught, as shown here, by the iron-jawed and long-clawed badger, an inveterate hunter and digger for reptiles as well as rodents and rabbits.

IN FOUR WEEKS the eaglet, whose crop is bulging from a recent feeding, weighs 46 ounces and has begun to sprout wings.

SIX WEEKS OLD, half-feathered and weighing some five pounds, the youngster wanders on ledges, though it cannot yet fly.

The Plight of Eagles

Where golden eagles build their eyries, on the sides of canyons and escarpments, no predator can disturb them except man. Eaglets are tended by both parents until 12 weeks old, when they are ready to fly. They are fed mainly on rabbits and squirrels—and occasionally on livestock. For these rare thefts, and the greater toll taken by eagles from the north

that spend the winter in the Southwest mountains, golden eagles have suffered heavily at the hands of ranchers. From 1941 to 1962, shoot-offs from planes destroyed about 20,000 eagles in West Texas and New Mexico alone. Not until then was the killing stopped by the enactment of a federal law, which may save the 3,000 to 5,000 pairs that still survive.

RIPPING OFF A LEG, AN ADULT GOLDEN EAGLE PREPARES TO EAT A RABBIT WHICH IT HAS BROUGHT TO THE EYRIE TO FEED ITSELF AND ITS YOUNG

A NEWLY HATCHED EAGLET, WEIGHING ONLY THREE OUNCES, LIES DOWNY AND HELPLESS WITH TINY TALONS CLENCHED

BYPASSING A BEAVER DAM, YOUNG PUMAS CROSS A STREAM IN SOUTHWESTERN COLORADO. LITTERMATES MAY STAY TOGETHER TWO YEARS

Fugitives in the Canyons

Most of North America's biggest and strongest cats, the pumas, or mountain lions, are today hiding out in the sparsely inhabited mountain valleys and canyons of the western United States and Canada. Here an estimated 8,000 to 13,000 live primarily on the abundant deer and smaller wild animals. In Utah and Nevada, their diet is 64 to 74 per cent mule deer, 20 per cent porcupines, and—in summer—15 per cent sheep. In terms of numbers, however, the pumas are now outclassed as pests by the flourishing coyotes. Bounties on pumas have been repealed in California, Washington, Oregon and British Columbia, and they are holding their own nearly everywhere, even spreading north into the Yukon.

A PROWLING PUMA, like the adult male above, is rarely seen: it is a silent and wary stalker. When within about 10 feet of a deer, it leaps on its victim and knocks it down, biting the back of its neck, thereby paralyzing or killing the animal. To kill a porcupine, the puma slips a paw under the unprotected belly, overturning and ripping open the prey at the same time.

The Sure-Footed Porcupine

Although the western porcupine also lives on the forested plains, it occurs in greatest numbers along the mountain ridges. Here it finds diverse plants to eat in summer, and here the wind is likely to keep the snow from piling deep in winter. Weak of eye, short of leg and slow in movement, the humpbacked porcupine nevertheless must be an adept climber to go after a mainstay in its diet, the inner bark of trees. It inches up trunks and follows its sensitive nose out along branches, gnawing off twigs that stand in its way or clinging with the relaxed ease of an acrobat to others seemingly too light for its body weight. When feeding, it sits or rears up on its haunches, strips or chips off the outer bark with its teeth and bites into the inner bark—often chewing so noisily it can be heard from 50 to 100 feet away.

AN ACCIDENTAL VICTIM, this deer shows what one swipe of a porcupine's tail can do. Each quill has barbs on it; moistened by blood, these expand and become anchored in the flesh.

THE PORCUPINE'S ARSENAL consists of some 20,000 to 30,000 sharp-tipped quills, which range in length from a mere two fifths of an inch on the cheeks to at least two inches on the tail.

Even babies have them and are born in sacs to protect the mother. Under the quills lies an insulating coat of brown fur, of which only the long, coarse guard hairs poke through here.

166

RESTING ON A CRAG, MOUNTAIN GOATS SEEM OBLIVIOUS TO THE PHOTOGRAPHER'S PRESENCE—ALL, THAT IS, BUT THE ONE-HORNED BILLY AT RIGHT.

King of the Mountain

Mountain goats are luckier than most North American animals in having a habitat of no real value to man and of such dizzying ruggedness as to intimidate most predators. For getting about in the stony heights, the mountain goat—which is actually not a goat at all but a type of antelope akin to the chamois —has specialized hoofs, the toes of which are concave and become suction cups when pressed down hard. Although a good jumper, the mountain goat is otherwise slow and deliberate in its movements. Scaling a cliff, it will stand up on its hind legs, place its front hoofs on the ledge above and muscle itself

BOTH MALES AND FEMALES HAVE HORNS, WHICH THOUGH SHORT AND BRITTLE, ARE DAGGER SHARP AND CAN INFLICT DEEP WOUNDS ON ATTACKERS

up, much as a careful mountaineer would do. If it has followed a narrow ledge to a dead end, it will rear up and turn slowly around until in a position to drop down on all fours and backtrack. Mountain goats are able to exist on twigs and buds and moss and lichens, but occasionally they are forced down from the heights when these foods grow in short supply, as in winter. They are protected year-round against the cold by thick, shaggy fur, with an undercoat so luxurious and fine that Indians of British Columbia gather this wool from bushes and the ground to weave blankets of cashmerelike softness.

A STURDY LAMB looks down on its mountain domain. Born in spring and nurtured on milk, tender foliage and flowers it will have grown nearly three quarters as tall as its mother by winter.

The Refugee

Another animal that dwells on the extreme heights is the bighorn sheep —but unlike the mountain goat, it seems to have been driven there by man. Once ranging from Alaska deep into Mexico, it was particularly numerous in the eastern foothills of the Rockies. Today it is found in almost inaccessible pockets, for as a hunter's prize the mountain sheep was hounded nearly to extinction, and where man failed to kill or displace it, his domestic animals often did by taking over its food supply. A magnificent beast, the bighorn has nonskid foot pads, a short coat and keen eyes. The males possess curling horns, which may be three or more feet in length. During the rut, contesting rams advance toward each other on hind legs, drop down, crouch—and crash into each other with such force that the sharp crack of their horns can be heard a mile away.

FATHER AND SON share a clump of grass. The adult's horns have much to say about its history—the intervals between the deep ridges that go all the way round indicate fat and lean years.

8

The Lost Frontiers

WE have seen that during the past four and a half centuries North America gradually became revealed to man as a major continent rather than as a peninsula of the Indies or as a mere island on the western ocean to Asia. The blankness of its map was filled in bit by bit, first by explorers, then by a dribble of pioneers, and finally by a wave of settlers. The peopling of North America represents a great epic in the modern annals of discovery and settlement—but from the naturalist's viewpoint it is a dreary sequence of events with little variation from one part of the continent to another. The pattern has been the same everywhere. First there was the wonder of discovery, of one major biome after another, each with its distinctive riches of landscape and unfettered animals to enchant, mystify and awe the beholder. Then there followed greed and reckless disregard; plant and animal communities that had developed over thousands of years were destroyed wholesale, often only in decades. Finally came the conservationists in the wake of the exploiters, culling through the devastation in despair, searching for stands of virgin trees, unplowed prairies, unspoiled shorelines and remnant animal populations that might preserve a portion of the original grandeur of the continent.

Now we stand at the end of the long wilderness road that has plowed through the great eastern forests, crossed the rippling sea of grasses, hurdled the great mountain barriers. The only extensive sweep of unspoiled America that remains is the northern roof of the continent, the coniferous forests and tundra of Canada and Alaska. There the mountain goats and sheep still stand statuesque on rocky crags; caribou herds still plod on their migrations; geese, ducks, swans and shorebirds still fill the sky above their summer nests. And there, too, are the havens of relatively large populations of animals that have been nearly extirpated in their once-flourishing ranges to the southward: grizzlies, wolves, wolverines, moose and others. For some species—whooping crane and musk ox—the northern frontier represents the last outpost of survival. The lamentable and senseless irony of man's tenure of the North American continent is that here, where he first invaded from Asia some 25,000 years ago, many kinds of animals are making their last stand against his presence.

Like other sections of the continent, the northern forests and tundra have also suffered under the heavy hand of man. But what makes this extensive area different is that it is still possible to save it. The northern roof represents both a challenge and an opportunity. Here we can demonstrate that mistakes made in the southern portions of North America have resulted in lessons belatedly learned. If we despoil these areas, we can no longer plead ignorance of the consequences; we cannot claim that there is more wilderness beyond the next mountain range or the next sea of grass, for this is where the wilderness ends.

The southern portion of this huge wilderness is known as the boreal or coniferous forest. Stretching from Newfoundland across Canada and into the interior of Alaska, it is the second largest forest left on the planet, exceeded only by the great forest of Siberia. Before the arrival of European man, it sent prongs into northern New England, down the spine of the Appalachians and around the Great Lakes, but these fringes have largely been cut over. As a whole, the forest has an over-all uniformity, thanks to its endless spires of spruce, balsam fir and pine. These are the three dominant kinds of conifers, but there are numerous other habitats as well—willows and birches along streams, and bogs with a flora of shrubs and flowering herbs. On the northern borders of the forest, the trees become increasingly stunted and scattered, and are gradually replaced by many kinds of grasses, herbs, sedges and heaths. This is the tundra.

THE tundra, or as it is sometimes called in North America, the "barren ground," might be likened to a grassland or a desert, but one that possesses special characteristics because it exists in the arctic regions. Although precipitation in the tundra is low—decreasing from about 20 inches a year to about 12 as one progresses northward—the evaporation rate is too. As a result, while water is generally scarce, it is at times overly abundant. The ground itself is permanently frozen down to bedrock, but during the brief summer of only two months the top few inches thaw out, and melting snow and ice suddenly fill the depressions in the rolling land, making the tundra glitter like fragments of a broken mirror in a quick-spreading mantle of greenery.

One might think that the inhospitable conditions that prevail in the north would make this land immune to the intrusions of modern man, but this has not been the case. Although the density of human population is, of course, much less there than in the southern portions of the continent, the coniferous forest and the tundra are being steadily penetrated by railroad lines and roads, by oil and mineral exploration crews, and by lumbermen who are chopping

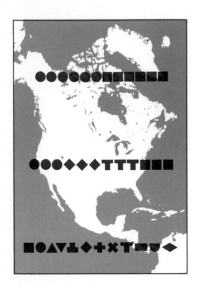

THE PATTERNS OF ANIMAL DISTRIBUTION

As the symbols on this map show in a highly simplified way, the numbers of different kinds of animals increase from the pole to the tropics, while the numbers of individual animals tend to decrease. Not surprisingly, this is largely a result of climate. In the arctic tundra, there are only a few niches for animals to occupy, and the prolonged cold so curtails the growing season that only a few types of plants exist for the herbivores to eat. Even so, populations expand radically here, coming to cyclic peaks because of the high reproductive rate among the animals, and then crashing because of stress, disease and famine. Predators are not numerous enough to keep these cyclical population explosions from occurring. In the tropics, there is a far greater diversity of animals, since so many more niches are available the year around. Population explosions fail to happen here, not only because of competition among the many herbivores and the presence of many kinds of predators to hunt them but also because the animals tend to have lower birth rates than northern species do.

their way ever northward. These intrusions are nothing new—French trappers were ranging widely throughout the coniferous forest by the middle of the 17th Century, and in 1670 the British set up the Hudson's Bay Company. At first the British trading posts were restricted to Hudson and James Bay, but soon their agents were bartering for furs with Indians and Eskimos throughout the evergreen woods and water-laced muskeg. Furs from animals here were superior to those obtained farther south; the cold climate encouraged thicker coats, and the shade of the dense forest kept them dark. The magnitude of the depletion of fur animals can be measured by some figures for 1743. In that year alone French traders bought about 170,000 beaver, marten, otter and fisher pelts. And the Hudson's Bay Company, in just one sale, disposed of the skins of 26,750 beavers, 14,730 martens and 1,850 wolves.

ALTHOUGH black bear, gray wolves and even trumpeter swans were trapped, the animals most sought were the family of carnivores known as Mustelidae—which includes the short-tailed weasel, or ermine, the otter, mink, pine marten, fisher and wolverine. Short-legged, long-bodied, agile and muscular, the mustelines are, pound for pound, possibly the most adept fighters on the continent and were well able to cope with their enemies until European man discovered the softness and beauty of their fur.

Most of them have fine bushy tails and wide short muzzles, giving them vaguely bearlike faces, and have the ability to emit a malodorous fluid. Each possesses its own distinctive habits. The pine marten, related to the Siberian sable and rivaling it for durability and softness of fur, is an expert aerialist, streaking through the treetops in pursuit of its prime food, the equally arboreal red squirrel. The short-tailed weasel possesses a supple body that can follow even meadow mice into their burrows. The mink lacks the weasel's speed on land but it can chase down fish and outfight muskrats in their own waters. The fisher, despite its name, is neither a water-lover nor a fisherman, though it will go after spawned-out salmon and eat dead fish or steal the catch of some other animal on occasion. It can attack a porcupine with impunity, flipping the quilled animal over on its back with a rapid flick of the paw and then ripping open the defenseless belly. It even attacks the pine marten in its own domain of the trees and can whip a dog experienced in hunting bears. Man, however, is everywhere with his traps and he is the one animal to whom the fisher easily succumbs—though even when caught in a trap, it may chew off its own imprisoned foot and hobble away. The fisher has, unfortunately for it, been one of the most highly regarded fur animals of all the mustelines, and this demand, together with loss of habitat through lumbering and fires, has made it a rare animal indeed. Probably only about 10,000 remain in all of Canada.

The mustelines are surprisingly small animals. The largest, and the one with the greatest reputation for ferocity even among this ferocious group, is the thick-bodied, stump-legged wolverine—much resembling a miniature bear with a skunklike smell. Not much more than three feet long, including eight inches of tail, and seldom weighing more than 35 pounds, it is nevertheless regarded as the demon of the north woods. It has been observed to chase bears, coyotes, even mountain lions from their kills, and then devour the prey itself. It is the despair of trappers because of its habit of following traplines to feed on captured animals. With its powerful jaw muscles and the unusual way in which the lower jaw fits into the upper, it can give a crushing bite out of all proportion to its small size; it has been known to kill caribou, mountain lions and deer.

During the summer, the lumbering wolverine is unable to run down its prey but must rely on carrion, bird eggs and even the larvae in wasp nests. But when snow lies deep on the ground, this creature is by far the swiftest of any other northern mammal. That is because its toes are widespread, allowing it to travel in deep powder snows, with relatively little effort, in a series of bounds. And its endurance is phenomenal; it can cover more than 40 miles without rest.

Judging from descriptions of those who have seen the animal, a wolverine loping across the snow-covered wilderness is a stirring sight, but it is also a rare one. Probably never very abundant in the first place, it has been heavily trapped by Eskimos because they prize the special qualities of its fur, which never hardens, even at freezing temperatures. It is virtually extinct south of the coniferous forest, except for remnant populations in the Sierras and Rockies. There are none in the "Wolverine State" of Michigan. Nor is it abundant even in Canada and Alaska; Ernest Thompson Seton reported seeing only two during his lifetime, and Adolph Murie, who spent a lifetime in the north woods, went for years without seeing one. In part this is because the wolverine is extremely wary and, informed of any danger through its keen senses, retreats, leaving only its broad tracks as a sign of its presence. Probably the only animal that the wolverine cannot cope with in direct combat is the porcupine; its clumsy attempts to flip it over on its back may even result in its own death from the quills that pierce its throat and stomach walls.

THE porcupine once abounded throughout the eastern forests, but now it is largely restricted to the coniferous forests of Alaska, Canada and their extensions southward in the western and northeastern United States. Its decreased numbers probably are due largely to loss of habitat, but it has also been persecuted by lumbermen because it is extremely destructive to trees. Not only does it forage in summer, but in winter it may stay eating in one tree for a week, propped in the crotches of branches and gorging on the bark and greenery until the tree stands nearly naked of needles. Sluggish and dull-eyed, the porcupine would probably occasion little more notice than any other rodent were it not for the uniqueness of its quills. The belief that it could send them flying like arrows arose early in the exploration of the continent. In 1672 one writer described this animal as "a very angry creature and dangerous, shooting a whole shower of quills." This belief, which of course is false, has become an imperishable legend of North American wildlife. The porcupine is continually shedding some of its 30,000 quills in the same way that any mammal is always losing some of its hairs. A quill that is about to be shed may become dislodged a bit sooner when the porcupine shakes itself in anger—but the quill is so lightweight and has so little momentum that it cannot travel more than a few feet. Nor can the animal determine the direction in which loose quills will fly.

The small, inconspicuous rodent or the even smaller insect feeding under the bark is ultimately important in the ecology of the northlands, but the spirit of this wilderness is captured most by the large mammals. For this is the domain of the great browsers. The most impressive of them all is the bull moose, which weighs upward of half a ton, carries huge palmate antlers and has a roaring call that is the loudest bellow of the north woods. The moose is one of the rare ungainly members of the graceful deer family. Its body is perched high on stiltlike legs, its upper lip droops over the lower, and its ears seem unnecessarily long. But all of these characteristics serve a purpose. As a browsing animal, its long legs enable it to travel through deep snow or the water of northern bogs and to obtain its browse from water plants and the high branches of trees. In summer a mature moose can trim branches to a height of nine feet; in winter, when it is elevated by snow on the ground, it can often reach branches 14 feet high, thus tapping a food resource no other animal can reach. And when it cannot reach the browse, it rides down the sapling between its forelegs, thus enabling it to feed on the top. Its overhanging lip looks much like that of the giraffe and serves the same purpose of enabling it to chomp on branches. And its long ears give it an acute sense of hearing, protection against its principal enemy, wolves. If attacked, it usually does not flee but instead lashes out with its sharp hoofs.

A decade or two ago it was feared by some conservationists that the moose was heading into extinction, or at least declining drastically; an estimate of its numbers less than 10 years ago showed a North American population of about 250,000 animals, almost all in the coniferous forests of Canada and Alaska. But these people did not understand the nature of this animal. To most people, the moose typifies the virgin spruce-fir forest, but this is not so. Its real habitat is the pockets of willow, aspen and birch surrounding bogs and places where fires or loggers have razed the mature forest, allowing secondary growth to prosper. Although its range has shrunk since primeval America, the surviving animals will probably hold their own, or even increase, as man continues to log and burn the coniferous forest.

The moose's equivalent in the tundra is the musk ox, but unlike the moose, it today totters on a razor's edge between extinction and survival. Where millions of musk ox once inhabited the northern portion of the continent, now only about 10,000 survive in a few areas across northern Canada to Greenland. A contributing factor to their downfall was a behavioral mechanism that under natural conditions had given them survival benefits. When attacked, their habit is to form a tight circle, heads downward and horns bristling outward. This defense worked well against wolves, but Eskimos armed with rifles found the compact and stationary herds easy targets.

The third large herbivore, the caribou, is the very symbol of the northland. It is gregarious, traveling in large herds, and also migratory, living in the tundra in summer and the coniferous forest in winter. These two behavioral characteristics work to balance each other out, for if the herds did not migrate they would quickly deplete their range of food plants, particularly lichens, which are slow to recover after overgrazing. And gregariousness, which, in a non-migratory animal, might be a drawback, aids survival against predators by providing many eyes and ears alert to danger and by the confusion to pursuers caused by a herd on the run. So vital an evolutionary factor has speed been that even a 10-day-old calf can keep up with a fleeing herd.

T HE name "caribou" comes from the Algonquian Indian word for "shoveler," reflecting the animal's habit of pawing the snow to uncover the vegetation beneath it. A comparative latecomer to the North American continent, the caribou probably crossed the Bering Strait land bridge only 75,000 years ago. Accompanying it on the great migration from Eurasia were numerous other large mammals, such as mammoths and woolly rhinoceroses, all now extinct, and the musk ox which is very nearly so. For many thousands of years, until the arrival of European man in North America, the caribou served as the cornerstone of the economy of the Chipewyan Indians, who stalked them with bows and arrows while disguised in caribou skins and antlers, and speared migrating caribou from boats. But these aboriginal human predators were too few in

THE VERSATILE MOOSE

Awkward-looking though it may be, the moose is actually an extremely efficient and well-adapted animal, able to provide itself with large supplies of food both winter and summer. When snow lies deep on the ground, the moose treads it down with its broad hoofs, building up a hard runway. This and its long legs enable it to reach branches as high as 14 feet from the ground (above). With the thaw, the moose takes to the lakes and wades in until its legs are fully submerged. Then its long neck and head allow it to browse on its favorite plant, the water lily (below).

SOME RAVAGING ALIENS

In a new habitat away from the checks of their natural predators and competitors, alien animals or plants may multiply prolifically, ravage the land, drive away native animals and thrive as pests, as the examples on these two pages show.

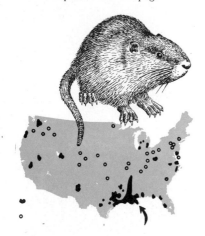

Imported from Argentina for their fur, nutria became pests in Louisiana when a few escaped and multiplied into a ravenous army that attacked cash crops. In Texas, where they were imported to control lake vegetation, five animals multiplied to more than 15,000 in five years. Since wild pelts are almost worthless, nutria are now fed to mink by breeders.

Starting as a minor flock of 100 released in Central Park in 1890, starlings have swarmed across the continent in clouds, their noisy numbers plaguing cities and farmers. In Idaho, an estimated three million starlings ate 12 tons of potatoes in eight hours. Wary and resistant, populations of starlings have survived trappings, poisonings and even dynamitings.

number and their hunting methods too crude to deplete the caribou herds. Looking back today, some naturalists think there were at least as many caribou as there were bison on the grasslands. As late as 1907 Ernest Thompson Seton estimated that about 30 million caribou still survived.

But no such numbers are found today. In this century the caribou has been losing out rapidly in its fight for survival, and recently the decline has been accelerating: the total North American population about a decade ago was estimated to be 726,000 animals and it is little more than half of that today. A woodland race of caribou once inhabited the mature forests of northeastern United States and eastern Canada, but it is exceedingly rare now except for remote parts of Canada. Overshooting probably contributed to the decline, but a more serious cause was the loss of habitat because of logging and fire, with the subsequent competition by white-tailed deer which invaded the cutover areas. The western races are virtually extinct south of the Canadian coniferous forest; it is estimated a scant 15 individuals survive in Washington and 100 in Idaho. Some of the decline has been due to excessive hunting for their skins, for bait and for dog food, but most of it has been destruction of habitat by fires and, as a further complication, the introduction of the related Eurasian reindeer into the North American tundra. This ill-advised idea was conceived in good will by a missionary who hoped to aid Eskimos reduced to starvation because the white man had killed off so many of their game animals. Between 1891 and 1902, some 1,300 domesticated reindeer were imported from Siberia, and they multiplied astronomically, greatly depleting the range on which caribou depend. And the Eskimos, used to hunting big grazers, showed little interest in herding them.

PREYING on the herds of caribou in particular, and to a lesser extent on other large mammals, is the wolf. Today we understand the ecology of the wolf and we know that it crops only the surplus and weakened animals. A wolf rarely can pull down a healthy adult caribou, but instead subsists on ailing adults and calves unable to keep up with the herd. The wolf's method of hunting caribou is to force a band that includes calves to run. The speed of the calves is almost, but not quite, as fast as that of the wolf. After a long chase, the weakest calf finally falters and gradually drops behind. This is the one the wolf gets. Wolves have not made deep inroads into the total caribou population and, in fact, by culling out the least fit calves, they have served to keep the herds vigorous.

But the pioneers, who feared attacks by wolves, and the settlers, who lost livestock to them, did not care about natural selection or the value of predators in the total wildlife community. They destroyed the wolf wherever they found it, and they found it almost everywhere, for the wolf was among the most widespread animals in North America, ranging throughout almost all of the land from the polar region southward to near Mexico City. The first bounty placed on the head of any animal in the New World was the offer, in 1630, of the Massachusetts Bay Company to pay a penny per wolf killed. The low rate of payment may indicate not so much New England parsimony as the great abundance of wolves. Shortly thereafter, many of the other colonies followed the lead of Massachusetts, and by 1800 the wolf was largely extinct in New England and eastern Canada, and in the early 1900s in the grasslands.

At first the unsuspicious wolves were easy to trap or poison, but those that survived the initial assault learned to avoid traps and bait. Some of these renegade wolves became legendary in their ability to avoid efforts to kill them. A South Dakota wolf, known as "Three Toes" because it had been maimed in escaping from traps, for 13 years eluded attempts by at least 150 men to kill it. Ranchers claimed that during this time it destroyed $50,000 worth of livestock. It was finally caught in 1925 by a professional hunter in the employ of the United States Government; he was presented with a gold watch by the grateful ranchers for his efforts in destroying one of the last wolves in the state.

One of the most famous wolves who embodied the essence of the wilderness was Lobo, the gigantic leader of a small band in New Mexico in the 1890s. Through cunning and audacity, Lobo for five years evaded every attempt to kill him by trap, poison or bullet. Ernest Thompson Seton finally trapped him by the ruse of playing on the wolf's well-known devotion to its family: Seton first captured the mate Blanca and then got Lobo when he came searching for her. But even in his moment of victory—as Lobo was firmly held by metal claws, with lassoes tight around his neck—Seton knew that the wolf was unvanquished. He could not bring himself to fire the final shot; instead he brought Lobo back to the ranch and secured him with a stout collar and chain. But Lobo showed no fear of his captors and he even disdained their food. Although robbed of his freedom, Lobo was the ultimate victor—he died as he had lived, with his eyes on the far canyons of his hunting territory.

One of the few blots on the impressive record of the national parks of the United States is that the wolf is the only animal to have been willfully eradicated from most of these lands set aside as havens for all living things. Mount McKinley National Park in Alaska is one of the few parks with a wolf population; a plan to eradicate them even there was narrowly averted about 20 years ago by a classic study of their ecology by Adolph Murie. Today the wolf has been exterminated from all settled portions of the continent. Only remnants of its northland populations, some isolated animals in Mexico, and limited numbers of the red wolf in Arkansas, Louisiana and eastern Texas still survive—mementos of man's efficiency in wiping a noble mammal from the landscape.

But even the last few surviving wolves are again being hounded by professional hunters, this time in defense of the dwindling caribou herds. When a recent survey in Canada revealed that caribou in the sweep of northland between Hudson Bay and the Mackenzie River had declined from 670,000 to about 275,000 in only seven years because, among many complex things, of wolf predation, Canadian authorities began a vigorous program of wolf killing by paid hunters. Within only five years, 4,000 wolves were eradicated about half of all that remained in this extensive area.

THIS recent threat to the wolf in Canada is but one small incident in the over-all wildlife picture of the continent. Yet it typifies the way we have too often responded to problems in conservation. We have been quick to eradicate, but slow to find difficult answers to difficult questions. The easy way is to play favorites—to kill the wolf that is killing the few caribou that survived killing by European man. This approach has marked our thinking about wildlife since the first settlers disembarked in a new world. It was fashionable only a few decades ago to shoot all birds of prey in the mistaken belief that the game birds, whose numbers had declined due to man's shooting, would then increase. The thing that is essentially wrong with playing favorites is that man is capricious and his fashions shift. Today's favorite may be tomorrow's bane.

The present century has seen in North America something new under the sun—an effort to repair and to save the wilderness. Fifty years ago, there were a few voices crying in the wilderness. Nowadays there is a loud and joyous

Of all the roadside flowers seen in the eastern United States, some 40 per cent are native to Europe, including the daisy, the field poppy and the dandelion. Another of the most common ones is Queen Anne's lace (above), a three-foot-high plant regarded as a pestiferous weed by farmers—but one which in domesticated form gave rise to the cultivated carrot.

The European gypsy moth, which first escaped from a Massachusetts laboratory in 1869, has inflicted millions of dollars of damage on eastern hardwoods. In the caterpillar stage, it feeds on 500 species of plants, but its spread has been slowed by spraying, trapping and strict interstate plant quarantines. In the 1930s WPA workers even killed moths by hand.

chorus crying for the wilderness, for protection of what remains after wantonness, greed and fear have run their course. Today vast amounts of energy and money are being expended to preserve from extinction the fewer than 30 whooping cranes, the condor, the eagle and the Key deer, even a stand of cypresses in a Florida swamp. Action has come late, but now it represents a determined effort to share the land with wildlife. One of our present tasks has been stated clearly by the Nature Conservancy: "We are obligated, as was Noah, to round up representatives of all living things, and see them safely through the flood—*the onrushing flood of civilization.*"

Yet, it seems that we are still searching for simple answers—or more properly, for principles. It is understandable that dramatic species like the whooping crane, the condor and the bison should have attracted mass concern to save them. But no upsurge of public protest calls for the preservation of less spectacular species whose prospects also are bleak—Bachman's warbler, Kirtland's warbler, the Cape Sable sparrow. And, of course, no voices are raised in defense of the obscure inhabitants of the continent—threatened salamanders in the Appalachians, nongame fishes in polluted rivers, even some of the humble rodents.

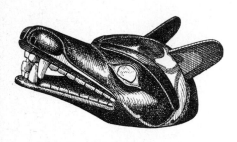

THE WOLF IN INDIAN ART

By contrast to European settlers, who brought to the New World their belief that the predatory wolf should be hunted to extermination, many American Indian tribes held this animal in reverence. The Indians of the northwest coast, for example, expressed their admiration for the strength and cunning of the wolf with rituals at which elaborately carved wolf masks were worn. Two of these masks are shown here. The top one was carved by the Tsimshians of British Columbia, the bottom one by the Makah of northwest Washington. One northwestern society felt it an honor if wolf spirits kidnaped their ancestors, and stylized wolf crests were prized in the same way that Europeans valued heraldic emblems.

THE modern science of ecology has allowed us to progress beyond simple preservation of endangered species. With this new knowledge, we now have it in our power to preserve the totality of the environment, not just the glamorous birds or mammals. Even more, we now better understand the complex interrelationships among living things, their food and shelter needs—and we may have it in our power actually to *re-create* primeval communities. In a small way, we have already made a start—Merriam's wild turkey has been restored to areas where it once lived in the mountains of New Mexico; 23 caribou have been flown from Newfoundland to Mount Katahdin, Maine, where they once flourished and where their food plants still grow. One sanctuary in Arizona, plagued by an abundance of rodents, has satisfied the denning needs of coyotes and enabled them to make a comeback in an area where they were virtually extinct, thus working to restore the balance of rodents again. If these things can be done, why cannot the wolf and the grizzly be transported from their retreats in the north and restored to the lands preserved by the Wilderness Bill? The possibilities of wilderness re-creation extend also to the humbler members of the ecological community. Where a link in a community's web of interlocking strands has been broken, the ecologist can step in—not to play favorites but solely to restore the age-old relationships.

Of course vigilance is still necessary to beat down any future raids on our resources or the mere disregard for the remnants of the primeval continent. We must continue to protest against pollution that turns aquatic communities into open sewers, unnecessary high dams that flood scenic and wild valleys, and soot that befouls the air. Surely we can afford the additional cost of routing new highways around wilderness areas, instead of through them. And we must constantly ask if it is necessary to continue federal predator control programs that kill nearly 200,000 animals a year, spending, for example $90,195 to put down coyotes in California which had destroyed $3,501 worth of sheep in 1962.

If these things are done, generations to follow will not lament that they were born too late to have known primeval America, to have seen the eagle course effortlessly through the sky, to have heard the mournful call of the coyote and the bellow of the moose, nor even to have watched a warbler construct a nest in the luxuriance of an unlogged forest.

SNUG IN NEW HAMPSHIRE'S HILLS, A TENTING GROUND CLUSTERS AROUND CAMPFIRES—CHROME, CONGESTION, RUBBER TIRES AND ALL

Our Parks: Wild Oases

Not all North America has been roughly handled by man. With rare insight, the national Government in the past hundred years has set aside enormous tracts of land, most of them in sparsely settled mountains and deserts, to be preserved as much as possible in their natural state. These are our National Parks—Yellowstone, Yosemite, Grand Canyon—memorials to a once mighty wilderness.

"For Public Use, Resort and Recreation"

In 1864, Congress used the words quoted above in setting aside the majestic, glacier-carved Yosemite Valley as a park, to be "inalienable for all time." Eight years later, a tract of over two million acres encompassing the headwaters of the Yellowstone River, remarkable for its spectacular geysers and hot springs, was likewise preserved. In the still unsettled West, a few men had become sufficiently aroused by the magnificence around them to try unselfishly to save some of it for future generations. The plan was to choose those places which were unique—wonderful works of nature like Yosemite with its granite cliffs or the falls and geysers of Yellowstone. But after the wave of settlement had swept west, wilderness itself became a rarity. Bison, elk and sequoia survived only where guns and axes were

not allowed. Thus the nation's system of parks plays a double role—as a gallery of natural wonders and, more important, a refuge for nature against humanity. Yet the parks' avowed purpose remains that of public use. Reconciling those contradictory themes has been the trying task of the National Park Service. Their solution will ever be a compromise, successful only with the help of the public.

FISHING BRIDGE in Yellowstone typifies a paradox: though seeking wilderness, park visitors like to congregate. Thus, in the most popular parks, crowds form and roads are jammed.

YOSEMITE TODAY is still the rock-girt valley of the 19th Century painting at left, but now its waters are inundated every summer by hordes of bright-clad swimmers and sunbathers.

A CENTURY AGO Yosemite Valley looked like this to the artist Albert Bierstadt as he watched the sun set behind El Capitan, one of the world's largest faces of bare granite. Cathedral Rocks tower opposite, while in the foreground, deer provide a scale for the heroic canvas.

183

The Canyon Country: Raw Material

The same water that cut the Grand Canyon sculptured a less colossal but more imaginative wonder of nature 254 miles upriver in Utah. Called the Canyon Country, it is a great plateau of fractured sandstone, roughly the size of Maine, fantastically eroded by water, wind and frost. Rugged and inhospitable, its deep twisting gorges and sheer cliffs alternate with hidden semiarid meadows and narrow box canyons, which seem to erupt in huge monoliths, soaring pinnacles and incredible vaulting arches— a maze which so far has held civilization at bay. This is the stuff parks are made of, and in 1964, after two years of debate, Congress passed a law setting aside some 258,000 acres of this land surrounding the confluence of the Green and Colorado Rivers to create Canyonlands National Park, so preserving one of the last sizable tracts of wilderness left in our West.

SEEKING ARTIFACTS, Bates Wilson, head of nearby Arches National Monument and a leader in the move to make Canyonlands a national park, inspects an old Indian storage cist.

THE NEEDLES, battlements and spires of rock banded in many colors, crowd the skyline of this high, dry country, accessible only in four-wheel-drive vehicles, on horseback or on foot.

THE WHITE RIM, a thick layer of hard, white sandstone overlying soft red rock, forms a wide shelf along the river canyon. In this case, the substrata has eroded away to leave a bridge.

TRAVERTINE TERRACES of Mammoth Hot Springs are among the wonders of Yellowstone caught by W. H. Jackson's camera in 1871. His pictures helped promote the national park idea.

THE GRIZZLY GIANT, a 3,500-year-old sequoia over 27 feet thick, has changed little since this picture was taken around 1860 with Galen Clark, Yosemite's first manager, at its foot.

CORNELIUS HEDGES

FERDINAND V. HAYDEN was sent by Congress to survey the Yellowstone area in 1871 before legislation was enacted to make it a park. Hayden (*seated, center*) also led this later group.

Conservation's Pioneers

It was Cornelius Hedges (*above*), a distinguished Montana judge and member of an expedition which explored Yellowstone in 1870, who first suggested that the entire area should be set aside as a national park. His view, expressed over a campfire, was greeted with approval, and at that moment, tradition has it, the concept of America's national parks was born. Like most traditions, it is only a partial truth. For one thing, six years earlier Congress had made a park of Yosemite, turning over the land to California. Moreover, the groundwork for Hedges' idea had been laid by many men before him. As early as 1833, George Catlin, the Indian-painter, made a similar plea for the forests around the Missouri River, and many after him had seconded the notion, though opposition in Washington grumbled that the federal Government was not in business to "raise wild animals." Nevertheless, after Yosemite and Yellowstone, the movement gathered momentum, and in 1916 the National Park Service was formed as a special agency of the Government to unify and administer the parks system—already large and destined to grow larger still.

PHILETUS W. NORRIS, Yellowstone's second chief, built the park's first roads. To enforce the game laws, he hired poacher Harry Yount, who proposed formation of a ranger service.

Gamekeepers and Custodians

When, in 1916, the public act creating the National Park Service finally brought all federal parks under a unified command, it also gave them a stated purpose: "To conserve the scenery and the natural and historic objects and the wildlife therein . . . by such means as will leave them unimpaired for the enjoyment of future generations." However, Congress did not accompany these lofty phrases with hard cash until 1918, and the main burden of policing the parks was carried as it had been—by the army. With money came the first National Park Service rangers, a force of 25 men under a chief ranger and four assistants. From that modest beginning the Service has branched out until today it employs nearly 600 rangers on a year-round basis, and more than twice that many during the summer. Their duties range from the purely custodial to rescue work, firefighting and the maintenance of an ecological balance among the parks' wild things. In addition, park naturalists, historians and archeologists, many of them recruited just for the summer from schools and colleges, help to make meaningful to the public the wonders preserved in their name.

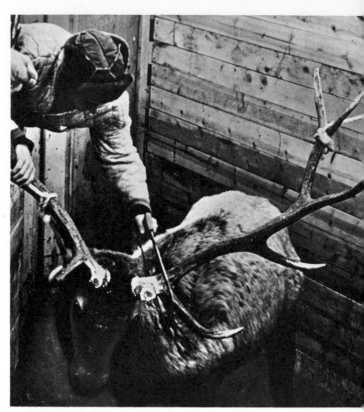

PREPARING ELK for group shipment to a less crowded range, a ranger saws off a bull's antlers to prevent its injuring its fellows. Such forced migration is necessary to halt overgrazing.

PRACTICING A DESCENT, two rangers seated in slings guide a stretcher with a simulated accident victim down a steep cliff. Drills like this are routine for rangers in mountainous areas.

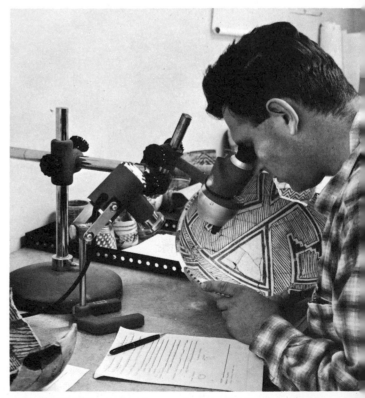

RECONSTRUCTING A RELIC, a park archeologist examines a pot with a microscope. These shards were from Mesa Verde park, more important for Indian remains than as wilderness.

188

HEAVING A BEAVER onto dry land, a ranger prepares to tag the trapped animal and release it. Knowledge of the habits of its resident wildlife is needed to properly administer a park.

TRANQUILIZING A BEAR in order to remove a can that somehow got stuck on its head, a ranger fires a drug-tipped arrow. The bear is quickly immobilized and awakens unharmed.

INTERPRETING NATURE, a park naturalist uses a portable microphone to address his audience on the rocky shore of Acadia National Park in Maine. He wears boots so that he can demonstrate his talk about the sea with living specimens from tidal pools. Similar talks, all free, are given on any summer day in all of the country's 108 national parks and monuments.

Beware of the Bears

DANGEROUS

DANGER OF THE BEARS was emphasized by this handbill distributed at Great Smoky Mountains National Park. But despite its warning, many people are still mauled each year.

Practically nothing gladdens the heart of a park tourist bent on embracing wilderness more than the sight of a black bear being friendly. All it seems to take is a small gratuity—a sandwich, say, or a bar of candy. The trouble is that, like any wild animal, park bears are unpredictable and for reasons unappreciated by the tourist they may suddenly turn vicious. They are responsible for nearly half of all the accidents of all kinds that take place in Yellowstone each year. Most wild animals, even in a sanctuary, maintain a healthy reluctance to mix with man. Not so the black bear. Being intelligent, omnivorous and lazy, it has adapted itself all too well to tourists' ways. It rifles campsites, loots improperly secured cars, even begs from the roadside; and when it does not get its way it may take a swipe at whatever is frustrating it. The best way to approach a bear, say Park Service rangers, is not to.

A SUDDEN CHARGE routs this camera-wielding tourist in the Great Smokies, who approached a black bear too closely in an effort to get a picture. There are cases known of mothers attempting to put children on the backs of bears to be photographed, or even of people approaching a bear cub despite its mother's growls. This man was lucky to escape a severe mauling.

FROM THE SAFETY OF THEIR BUS, SUMMER EMPLOYEES AT YELLOWSTONE GREET AN OLD FRIEND WITH HER NEW CUB

OLYMPIC
NAT'L. PK.

MT.
RAINIER
NAT'L. PK. **WASH.**

GLACIER
NAT'L. PK.

C A N A D A

MONT.

THEODORE
ROOSEVELT
NAT'L. MEM. PK.

N. DAK.

CRATER LAKE
NAT'L. PK.

OREG.

CRATERS OF
THE MOON
NAT'L. MON.

IDAHO

DEVIL'S TOWER
NAT'L. MON.

YELLOWSTONE
NAT'L. PK.

WIND
CAVE
NAT'L. PK.

S. DAK.

BADLANDS
NAT'L. MON.

OREGON CAVES
NAT'L. MON.

LASSEN
VOLCANIC
NAT'L. PK.

GRAND
TETON
NAT'L. PK.

WYO.

MUIR WOODS
NAT'L. MON.

NEV.

UTAH

DINOSAUR
NAT'L. MON.

NEBR.

CALIF.

DEVIL'S POSTPILE
NAT'L. MON.

ARCHES
NAT'L
MON.

CANYONLANDS
NAT'L. PK.

ROCKY
MOUNTAIN
NAT'L. PK.

YOSEMITE
NAT'L. PK.

SEQUOIA AND
KINGS CANYON
NAT'L. PKS.

CEDAR
BREAKS
NAT'L.
MON.

BRYCE
CANYON
NAT'L. PK.

CAPITOL
REEF
NAT'L. MON.

ZION
NAT'L. PK.

NATURAL
BRIDGES
NAT'L. MON.

COLO.

GREAT SAND
DUNES
NAT'L. MON.

KANS.

PINNACLES
NAT'L. MON.

DEATH VALLEY
NAT'L. MON.

JOSHUA TREE
NAT'L. MON.

GRAND
CANYON
NAT'L. PK.
AND
MON.

RAINBOW
BRIDGE
NAT'L.
MON.

MESA
VERDE
NAT'L. PK.

PETRIFIED FOREST
NAT'L. PK.

CHANNEL ISLANDS
NAT'L. MON.

ARIZ.

ORGAN PIPE
CACTUS NAT'L. MON.

SUNSET CRATER
NAT'L. MON.

N. MEX.

OKLA.

PLATT
NAT'L.
PK.

SAGUARO NAT'L.
MON.

WHITE SANDS
NAT'L. MON.

CHIRICAHUA
NAT'L. MON.

CARLSBAD CAVERNS
NAT'L. PK.

TEXAS

ALASKA

MT. McKINLEY
NAT'L. PK.

C A N A D A

BIG BEND NAT'L. PK.

KATMAI
NAT'L. MON.

GLACIER BAY
NAT'L. MON.

M E X I C O

OF THE 201 AREAS ADMINISTERED BY THE NATIONAL PARK SERVICE, 59 OF THE MOST INTERESTING FROM THE VIEWPOINT OF THEIR LAND

A

ISLE ROYALE
NAT'L. PK.

L. Superior

ME.

ACADIA
NAT'L. PK.

MINN.

L. Michigan

L. Huron

VT.

N.H.

CAPE COD
NAT'L. SEASHORE

WIS.

MICH.

L. Ontario

N.Y.

MASS.

CONN. R.I.

Mississippi River

EFFIGY MOUNDS
NAT'L. MON.

L. Erie

PA.

N.J.

FIRE ISLAND
NAT'L. SEASHORE

IOWA

INDIANA
DUNES NAT'L. PK.
(Proposed)

OHIO

MD.

DEL.

Missouri River

ILL.

IND.

SHENANDOAH
NAT'L. PK.

W. VA.

VA.

Ohio River

MAMMOTH CAVE
NAT'L PK.

MO.

KY.

CAPE HATTERAS
NAT'L. SEASHORE

GREAT SMOKY
MTS. NAT'L. PK.

TENN.

N.C.

ARK.

S.C.

**UNITED STATES
PARKS AND RESERVES**

HOT SPRINGS
NAT'L. PK.

MISS.

ALA.

National Wildlife Refuges

National Parks and Monuments

GA.

Indian Reservations

National Forests

LA.

0   50   100   150   MILES

FLA.

EVERGLADES
NAT'L. PK.

Appendix
The National Parks of North America

Here are short descriptions of the principal national parks and national monuments of the United States and Canada. The first figure given for each park is its size in acres, the next is the date it was officially created. The small symbols, indicating some of the facilities available, are identified in the key directly above.

Alaska
GLACIER BAY N.M.
(2,274,248) 1925. ⚹ Ⓖ ⬥

Giant glaciers, both creeping and stagnant, are fringed by postglacial land varying from bare rock to dense forest. Bears and deer abound, while seals and whales swim in the bay.

KATMAI N.M.
(2,697,590) 1918. ⚹ Ⓖ

The largest area under National Park Service administration. Its habitats range from Hudsonian spruce forest to arctic tundra grass. Bears and caribou are common. In one area, the Valley of 10,000 Smokes, hot gases rise from fissures in volcanic rock.

MOUNT McKINLEY N.P.
(1,939,354) 1917. ⚹ ▲

Named for the highest peak in North America, this is a park of tundra, with only occasional dwarf spruce. Caribou and willow ptarmigan are common.

Arizona
CHIRICAHUA N.M.
(10,481) 1924. ⚹ ▲

A volcanic area now eroded into stunning monoliths. This mountain park was once the stronghold of the Apache Indian chief Cochise. Its forests of pine and scrub oak harbor many unusual species of animal life.

GRAND CANYON N.P.
(673,203) 1919. ⚹ ▲

Legendary for its beauty, the Grand Canyon is also literally a slice through the geological past, with plant and animal fossils exposed in its layers. From top to bottom, the canyon contains five different life zones, each with its own plants and animals.

ORGAN PIPE N.M.
(328,691) 1937. ⚹ ▲

This Sonoran desert region, with organ pipe, saguaro and Wislizenius barrel cactuses and other arid land plants, is one of the last refuges of the desert bighorn sheep.

PETRIFIED FOREST N.P.
(92,752) 1962. ⚹

Set near the Painted Desert, a section of brilliantly colored badlands, worn by time into dramatic shapes, with petrified trees exposed by erosion scattered on the desert floor.

SAGUARO N.M.
(60,987) 1933. ⚹

Lofty saguaro cactuses, sometimes 50 feet tall, dominate this park, which is also the home of such desert species as the gilded flicker, the white-tailed deer and *Lysiloma*, a shrub found nowhere else in the U.S.

SUNSET CRATER N.M.
(3,040) 1930. ⚹

Red and orange cinders cap a 1,000-foot-high volcanic cone, dotted by gnarled ponderosa pine and the Arizona red gilia.

Arkansas
HOT SPRINGS N.P.
(989) 1921. ⚹ ▲ ▽ Ⓖ ⬥

A million gallons of mineral water, with a constant average temperature of over 143°, bubble from 47 springs here every day of the year.

California
CHANNEL ISLANDS N.M.
(18,167) 1938. ▲ ▽ Ⓖ ⬥

These two small rugged islands are sanctuaries for sea lions and sea birds and are also the habitat of certain rare flowering plants. Fossils of Pleistocene elephants have been found here.

DEATH VALLEY N.M.
(1,763,848) 1933. ⚹ ▲ ▽

The lowest spot in the Western Hemisphere (282 feet below sea level), this is a park of sand, salt flats and volcanic craters rimmed by spectacular desert mountains. Coyotes, kangaroo rats and roadrunners live here, also a plant seen nowhere else—rocklady.

DEVILS POSTPILE N.M.
(798) 1911. ⚹ ▲

Blue-gray basaltic columns, up to 60 feet tall, are fitted together like pipes of an organ to build a sheer 300-foot wall. Rainbow Falls, nearby, is one of the West's handsomest.

JOSHUA TREE N.M.
(504,700) 1936. ⚹ ▲

A member of the lily family that grows up to 40 feet high, the Joshua tree is preserved here in a desert mountain setting. Under its angular limbs live mule deer, badgers and foxes, along with more than 230 bird species.

KINGS CANYON N.P.
(453,768) 1940. ⚹ ▲ Ⓖ ⚡

Gigantic canyons meet here in the most rugged portion of the Sierra Nevada, where lofty peaks and granite domes rise behind alpine lakes and stands of giant sequoias.

LASSEN VOLCANIC N.P.
(105,106) 1916. ⚹ ▲ ▽ Ⓖ ⬥ ⚡

The last volcano to erupt in the continental U.S., Lassen Peak was active between 1914 and 1921, leaving stark and strange lava forms. Most of the park is still verdant forest, and its lakes are a resting point for migrating fowl.

MUIR WOODS N.M.
(485) 1908. ⚹

Often taller than the giant sequoias, but with thinner trunks, redwoods grow 300 feet high here in a dense virgin grove, providing a habitat for black-tail deer, gray fox and wildcat.

PINNACLES N.M.
(13,618) 1908. ⚹ ▲

Volcanic domes and spires up to 1,200 feet tall originate on the floors of deep, narrow canyons, often pierced by caves.

SEQUOIA N.P.
(385,419) 1890. ⚹ ▲ Ⓖ ⚡

Huge groves in which are clustered at least a million giant sequoias are scattered across the western half of this park. The eastern half has inspiring mountain landscapes with deep gorges and high peaks including Mount Whitney, highest in the U.S. outside of Alaska.

YOSEMITE N.P.
(758,041) 1890. ⚹ ▲ ▽ Ⓖ ⚡

The "incomparable valley," with its forested floor and towering cliffs, has some of the highest waterfalls on earth, a sequoia with a road tunneled through it, more than 300 lakes, five zones with 220 bird and 75 mammal species.

Colorado
DINOSAUR N.M.
(190,962) 1915. ⚹ ▲

The bones of 12 species of dinosaurs have been unearthed here in a region folded and tilted by repeated movements of the earth's crust. Wind rain and stream erosion have exposed colorful rock layers millions of years old. Here too are the spectacular canyons of the Yampa and Green Rivers.

GREAT SAND DUNES N.M.
(34,980) 1932. ⚹ ▲

Sand dumped by westerly winds has formed dunes up to 1,000 feet high—probably the highest in the U.S.—in a dramatic setting at the foot of the lofty Sangre de Cristo Range. A river that disappears into the silica dunes gives life to only one plant, the sunflower.

MESA VERDE N.P.
(51,018) 1906. ⚹ ▲

In the canyons of a tree-covered mesa, built into cliffside caves, stand the largest discovered ruins of the ancient Pueblo Indians.

ROCKY MOUNTAIN N.P.
(256,310) 1915. ▲ Ⓖ ⬥ ⚡

The highest continuous auto road in the U.S., reaching an altitude of 12,183 feet, provides vistas of one of the most scenic sections of the Colorado Rockies. In these mountains, which include 65 named peaks over 10,000 feet, roam mountain sheep and American elk.

Florida
EVERGLADES N.P.
(1,301,327) 1947. ⚹ ▲ Ⓖ ⬥

The only place in the continental U.S. touched by the tropical life zone, this park is a wilderness of Everglades prairies, royal palms, salt and fresh watercourses and is said to have the greatest mangrove forests in North or South America. Bird life is spectacularly varied and abundant. Manatees, porpoises and alligators may be seen.

Idaho
CRATERS OF THE MOON N.M.
(48,004) 1924. ⚹ ▲

No other area has such a concentration of

volcanic features. Craters, cinder cones, lava flows, caves and tunnels are found, with only lichen and a few other hardy plants for flora.

Iowa
EFFIGY MOUNDS N.M.
(1,204) 1949. ⚭

Burial mounds of the Midwestern Indians here are surmounted by figures carved in dirt.

Kentucky
MAMMOTH CAVE N.P.
(50,696) 1936. ⚭ C

A labyrinth of tunnels, underground streams, pits and vaulted chambers, this is part of the largest cave system in the world, 150 miles of which have been explored. Some of the caves contain sightless crawfish, beetles and fishes.

Maine
ACADIA N.P.
(30,944) 1919. ⚭ ▲ ▽ C ⛁

Land and sea life overlap here on a scenic coast dominated by Cadillac Mountain, highest point on the Atlantic shore. Tide pools, sea caves, islands, bays, lakes, verdant forests and a variety of bird life are displayed.

Massachusetts
CAPE COD NATIONAL SEASHORE
(26,666) 1961. ⚭ ▲ ▽ C ⛁

The results of sea and glacial action upon a land mass can be seen here on white beaches with dunes and cliffs along 40 miles of coastline, a haven for native and migratory birds.

Michigan
ISLE ROYALE N.P.
(539,339) 1940. ⚭ ▲ C ⛁

Untouched wilderness, this roadless park, 50 miles offshore in Lake Superior, can be reached only by boat. It has 36 kinds of orchids, 83 inland lakes with 46 fish species and a moose population living in balance with predatory wolves. On the beaches are greenstones—rare pebbles found only here.

Montana
GLACIER N.P.
(1,009,111) 1910. ⚭ ▲ C ⛁

Some 50 small glaciers and 200 narrow lakes are scattered through a magnificent mountain wilderness of forest, wild-flower gardens and towering peaks. In 1932, this and adjoining Waterton Lakes Park in Canada were proclaimed an International Peace Park.

New Mexico
CARLSBAD CAVERNS N.P.
(45,847) 1930. ⚭

Twenty miles of chambers are linked here in the world's largest limestone caverns, the deepest about 1,000 feet down. Several million bats live in the caves.

WHITE SANDS N.M.
(140,247) 1933. ⚭

This is the largest gypsum sand desert in the world, with more than 300,000 acres of pure white dunes.

Oklahoma
PLATT N.P.
(912) 1906. ⚭ ▲ ▽ C

No two of the 32 springs at this smallest of all U.S. national parks have the same mineral content. Five million gallons of water flow daily from two springs alone.

Oregon
CRATER LAKE N.P.
(160,290) 1902. ⚭ ▲ C ⛁ ⚡

Contains the deepest lake (1,996 feet) in the

U.S., formed by an immense volcanic crater over six miles across. Around its edge is the rugged crater rim which supports a dense forest containing 570 flowering plant species.

South Dakota
BADLANDS N.M.
(99,986) 1939. ⚭ ▲

Rapid erosion has carved the fabled Badlands from soft layers of rock into myriads of buttes and color-banded spires, and in the process revealed the fossil bones of many long-extinct mammals. Prairie rodents and birds live here among prickly pear and yucca.

WIND CAVE N.P.
(28,053) 1903. ⚭ ▲

To equalize the air pressure inside this 10-mile-long cave with that outside, wind blows either in or out depending on atmospheric changes, while nearby pronghorn antelope and bison graze on the pine-studded prairie.

Tennessee
GREAT SMOKY MOUNTAINS N.P.
(236,079) 1930. ⚭ ▲ C

This unspoiled wilderness in the highest mountain range in the eastern U.S. is a nature lover's delight, in recent years attracting more visitors than any other park. Here stands the finest hardwood forest in the country, with 140 varieties of trees, the natural home of scores of birds and wildlife species and many hundreds of wild flowers.

Texas
BIG BEND N.P.
(700,220) 1944. ⚭ ▲ C

Cut by canyons and punctuated by mountains, the dry plain here abounds with desert flora and fauna, including the scarce blue-throated hummingbird. Rich in fossil beds, Big Bend once yielded a clam shell three feet by four feet.

Utah
ARCHES N.M.
(34,250) 1929. ⚭ ▲

Set among red sandstone domes, spires, fins and other odd rock forms are over 80 natural stone arches, more than in any other section of the U.S. The king of these spans 291 feet and is the longest in the world.

BRYCE CANYON N.P.
(36,010) 1928. ⚭ ▲

One of the most astonishing sights of the continent, this bowl-shaped area embraces a myriad of brightly colored rock formations, sculptured by weather erosion into fantastic columns and spires.

ZION N.P.
(132,470) 1919. ⚭ ▲ ▽ C

Here, forested tableland, almost 8,000 feet high, is crisscrossed with deep, narrow canyons and towering sandstone formations.

Virginia
SHENANDOAH N.P.
(193,178) 1935. ⚭ ▲ C

An Appalachian wilderness, most of this park is 2,000 feet above sea level, with a wealth of flowering plants, birds and mammals. An automobile road, the Skyline Drive, runs along the high ridges for 105 miles.

Washington
MOUNT RAINIER N.P.
(241,571) 1899. ⚭ ▲ C ⚡

The lofty ancient volcano of Mount Rainier is cloaked by 12 major glaciers up to 500 feet thick. Below, deep forests give way to lush

meadows with profusions of wild flowers.

OLYMPIC N.P.
(888,558) 1938. ⚭ ▲ C ⚡

Under rugged snow-capped mountain peaks, the great Olympic rain forest flourishes with Sitka spruce and hemlock 200 feet tall, draped with club moss. On the floor grow ferns and mosses. Offshore, seals and sea lions swim.

Wyoming
DEVILS TOWER N.M.
(1,267) 1906. ⚭ ▲

The first scenic wonder to be proclaimed a national monument. All that remains of a dome-shaped mass of earth pushed up by lava is the so-called tower—the lava core itself—865 feet high. A colony of prairie dogs, one of the last in existence, lives nearby.

GRAND TETON N.P.
(302,255) 1929. ▲ ▽ C ⛁

Formed by faulting, the Tetons rise abruptly and uncluttered by foothills from Jackson Hole, the scenic valley at the eastern base of the range. Elk, moose and beaver roam this scenically dramatic region, and in some of its clear lakes nest rare trumpeter swans.

YELLOWSTONE N.P.
(2,213,207) 1872. ⚭ ▲ C ⛁

Once a volcanic land, this first and largest national park contains 3,000 geysers, more than any comparable area in the world. Ninety per cent forested today, the park has at least 1,000 miles of trails, which run up mountains, past lakes and streams, and place all aspects of the area's rich animal life on view.

Canadian National Parks
BANFF N.P., ALBERTA
(1,640,960) 1885. ▲ ▽ C ⛁ ⚡

Mountain ranges, one behind the other, rise in this, the oldest of Canada's national parks. Forests and flowers, and a rich assortment of animals border vast ice fields, one of which covers 150 square miles.

CAPE BRETON HIGHLANDS N.P., NOVA SCOTIA
(249,600) 1936. ▲ ▽ C

Placed between the Atlantic Ocean and the Gulf of St. Lawrence, this park forms part of a tableland which extends to the sea in towering headlands cut by gorges and valleys.

FUNDY N.P., NEW BRUNSWICK
(50,880) 1948. ▲ ▽ C

Some of the world's highest tides (over 60 feet) swoop into the Bay of Fundy and have carved the sandstone cliffs into rock forms. Rising in steps from the bay, the land becomes forested at 1,000 feet, while inland are maple groves.

JASPER N.P., ALBERTA
(2,688,000) 1907. ▲ ▽ C ⛁ ⚡

Snow-capped summits form a sea of peaks here on the eastern slope of the Canadian Rockies.

KOOTENAY N.P., BRITISH COLUMBIA
(347,620) 1920. ▲ C

Deep canyons, high waterfalls, an iceberg lake and mineral hot springs are all here on the western slope of the Canadian Rockies, together with moose, elk, bears, Rocky mountain goats and cougars.

PRINCE ALBERT N.P., SASKATCHEWAN
(957,440) 1927. ⚭ ▲ ▽ C ⛁

A park of dense forest and hundreds of lakes, many with white sand beaches. American white pelicans and cormorants inhabit the area in large numbers.

195

Credits

The sources for the illustrations in this book are shown below.

Credits for pictures from left to right are separated by commas, top to bottom by dashes.

Cover—Willis Peterson
8, 9—George Hunter
11—map by Elmer Smith
14, 15—map and drawings by Otto van Eersel based on material courtesy the Indiana Historical Society
17—Josef Muench
18, 19—map by Adolph E. Brotman, Esther Henderson from Rapho-Guillumette
20, 21—map by Adolph E. Brotman, Bradley Smith from Photo Researchers, Inc.
22, 23—map by Adolph E. Brotman—Bradley Smith from Photo Researchers, Inc.
24, 25—map by Adolph E. Brotman, Grant Heilman
26, 27—Ray Atkeson, map by Adolph E. Brotman
28—George Silk
32, 33—drawings by Enid Kotchnig
34, 35—drawings by Guy J. Coheleach
37—drawings by John Schoenherr
39—Lionel Murphy
40—Fritz Goro—Robert Meyerriecks (2)
41—Gordon S. Smith—Robert Meyerriecks (2)
42, 43—Kosti Ruohomaa from Black Star, Robert Morton—Annan Photo Features
44—Edward S. Ross
45 through 49—paintings by Walter Linsenmaier
50—Chuck Abbott from Rapho-Guillumette
55—drawings by John Schoenherr
56, 57—drawings and maps by Otto van Eersel

58—drawings by Guy J. Coheleach
60—drawing by Otto van Eersel
61—Richard Erdoes
62, 63—map by David Greenspan
64 through 66—Peter Stackpole
67—Eliot Elisofon from the collections in the Museum of New Mexico
68, 69—Eliot Elisofon except bottom right Horace Bristol
70, 71—Paul Jensen—Eliot Elisofon, Charles Herbert from Photo Researchers, Inc.
72, 73—The Smithsonian Institution
74—Walter Dawn
76—drawing by Otto van Eersel
78—drawings by Barbara Wolff
79—drawings by Enid Kotchnig
81—drawing by Gaetano DiPalma
83—Walter Dawn
84, 85—Walter Dawn, Dmitri Kessel
86, 87—Walter Dawn
88, 89—Walter Dawn except right Jack Dermid
90, 91—Kenneth W. Fink except top left Walter Dawn
92, 93—Jack Dermid—D. J. Nelson from National Audubon Society
94—Andy Russell & Sons, courtesy of the Taplin Fund and the New York Zoological Society
96—drawing by John Schoenherr
100—drawing by Enid Kotchnig
103—Grant Heilman
104, 105—maps and drawings by Matt Greene
106, 107—left Eliot Porter; right R. W. Mitchell, Rutherford

Platt—David R. Bridge—Walter Dawn, Oscar B. Greenleaf
108, 109—Andy Russell & Sons, courtesy of the Taplin Fund and the New York Zoological Society; George Silk
110—Willis Peterson
111—Jack Dermid
112 through 115—C. P. Fox
116, 117—Paul Jensen
119—drawing by Elmer Smith
121—drawing by Enid Kotchnig
124, 125—drawings by Otto van Eersel
127—Paul Jensen
128 through 135—paintings by Jay Matternes photographed by Henry Beville courtesy the Smithsonian Institution; key drawings by Otto van Eersel
136, 137—Joe Van Wormer from Photo Researchers, Inc. except bottom George Silk
138—Joe Van Wormer from Photo Researchers, Inc.
139—Carl Iwasaki—Hansel Mieth
140, 141—Ed Park except top Joe Van Wormer from Photo Researchers, Inc.
142, 143—Dewey Bergquist from Monkmeyer Press Photos
144, 145—Richard Erdoes
146—drawings by Enid Kotchnig
148—drawings by Enid Kotchnig
151—drawing by John Schoenherr
155 through 161—Shelley Grossman
162—Robert W. Mitchell
163—Robert W. Mitchell (2)—George Silk
164—W. L. Miller from National Audubon Society

165—Verna R. Johnston
166—James Simon from Photo Researchers, Inc.—Lee Boltin
167—Ed Park
168, 169—Kenneth W. Fink
170, 171—Kenneth W. Fink, William W. Bacon III from Rapho-Guillumette
172—National Park Service Photo
174—map by Gaetano DiPalma
177—drawings by John Schoenherr
178, 179—drawings and maps by Otto van Eersel
180—drawings by Enid Kotchnig
181—Albert Fenn
182, 183—Jon Brenneis except left Herbert Orth courtesy Museum of Fine Arts, Boston. M. & M. Karolik Collection
184—Paul Jensen
185—National Park Service Photos
186—Yellowstone National Park Photo—National Park Service Photo
187—National Park Service Photos except bottom right Yellowstone National Park Photo
188—National Park Service Photos except top right Yellowstone National Park Photo by Wayne Replogle
189—National Park Service Photo, Yellowstone National Park Photo by Wayne Replogle—Robert Morton
190—Henry Groskinsky—National Park Service Photo
191—Carl Iwasaki
194, 195—map by Bill Dove
Back cover drawing by Otto van Eersel

Acknowledgments

The editors of this book are particularly indebted to Richard G. Van Gelder, Chairman and Associate Curator, Department of Mammalogy, The American Museum of Natural History, and Roger Tory Peterson, who read the text in its entirety. They also want to thank Sydney Anderson, Associate Curator, Department of Mammalogy, The American Museum of Natural History; James W. Atz, Editor and Research Associate, Bingham Oceanographic Laboratories, Yale University; Winston E. Banko, Director, Pacific Project, Division of Birds, Smithsonian Institution; John E. Bardach, Professor of Fisheries and Zoology, University of Michigan; Louis R. Binford, Assistant Professor of Anthropology, University of Chicago; François Bourlière, Professor, Faculté de Médicine de Paris; Victor Cahalane, Assistant Director, New York State Museum; Sture T. Carlson, Chief, Branch of Park Protection, National Park Service; Cheyenne Mountain Zoo, Colorado Springs; Roland C. Clement, Staff Biologist, National Audubon Society; D. B. Coombs, Regional Director, National Parks Branch, Department of Northern Affairs and National Resources, Canada; Benjamin Davidson, Associate Professor of Meteorology, New York University; Joseph A. Davis Jr., Curator of Mammals, New York Zoological Park; Frederick J. Dockstader, Director, Museum of the American Indian, Heye Foundation; Herndon Dowling, Curator of Reptiles, New York Zoological Park; Wilbur E. Dutton, Photographic Research Assistant, National Park Service; Harold J. Grant Jr., Chairman, Department of Insects, Academy of Natural Sciences of Philadelphia; John A. Guinan, Information Officer, United States Fish and Wildlife Service; Lawrence Hadley, Chief of Information, National Park Service; John N. Hamlet; James R. Harlan, Conservation Consultant, Department of Health, Education and Welfare; Sidney Horenstein, Scientific Assistant, Department of Fossil Invertebrates, The American Museum of Natural History; Richard M. Klein, Curator of Plant Physiology, New York Botanical Garden; The May Natural History Museum of the Tropics, Colorado Springs; Robert Jones, Senior Librarian, New York Botanical Garden; Robert Mitchell, Department of Zoology, University of Texas; Charles Most, Chief, Current News Section, Office of Information, United States Fish and Wildlife Service; William S. Osburn Jr., Associate Director, Institute of Arctic and Alpine Research, University of Colorado; W. Leslie Robinette, Chief, Section Upland Ecology, Bureau of Sport Fisheries and Wildlife, United States Department of the Interior; Edward S. Ross, Curator, Department of Entomology, California Academy of Sciences, San Francisco; Rodney Royce, Biologist, Olympic National Park; Gerald L. Shak, Principal Assistant, United States Weather Bureau; Eric Schneider, Lamont Geological Observatory, Columbia University; Walter B. Spofford, Associate Professor of Anatomy, State University Hospital of Upstate Medical Center, Syracuse University; John Townsley, Superintendent, New York City National Park Service Group; Cecil Williams, Federal Research Center, United States Fish and Wildlife Service; M. Woodbridge Williams, Acting Chief, Branch of Still Pictures, National Park Service; Bates Wilson, Superintendent, Arches National Monument, Moab, Utah; and the library staff of The American Museum of Natural History.

Bibliography

Geography and Regional Descriptions

*Carson, Rachel, *The Edge of the Sea*. Houghton Mifflin, 1955.

Chapman, V. J., *Salt Marshes and Salt Deserts of the World*. Interscience, 1960.

Farb, Peter, *Face of North America*. Harper & Row, 1963.

Fenneman, Nevin M., *Physiography of Eastern United States*. McGraw-Hill, 1948. *Physiography of Western United States*. McGraw-Hill, 1931.

Hay, John, *The Great Beach*. Doubleday, 1963.

Ise, John, *Our National Park Policy*. Johns Hopkins Press, 1961.

Jaeger, Edmund C., *The North American Deserts*. Stanford University Press, 1957.

*Murie, Adolph, *A Naturalist in Alaska*. Devin-Adair, 1961.

Ricketts, Edward F., and Jack Calvin, *Between Pacific Tides* (rev. ed.). Stanford University Press, 1962.

Shimer, John A., *This Sculptured Earth*. Columbia University Press, 1959.

Stamp, L. Dudley, *A Regional Geography, Part 1: The Americas* (10th ed.). John Wiley & Sons, 1962.

Thomson, Betty Flanders, *The Changing Face of New England*. Macmillan, 1958.

†Tilden, Freeman, *The National Parks* (rev. ed.). Alfred A. Knopf, 1954.

Weaver, J. E., *North American Prairie*. Johnsen, 1954.

*Webb, Walter Prescott, *The Great Plains*. Ginn and Company, 1931.

Explorers of America

**Bakeless, John, *The Eyes of Discovery*. Dover, 1961.

†Brebner, John B., *The Explorers of North America, 1492-1806*. Meridian, 1964.

*Cruickshank, Helen Gere, ed., *John and William Bartram's America*. Devin-Adair, 1957.

*DeVoto, Bernard, *The Course of Empire*. Houghton Mifflin, 1952.

Hodge, Frederick, and Theodore H. Lewis, eds., *Spanish Explorers in the Southern United States, 1528-1543*. Barnes & Noble, reprint 1959.

Horgan, Paul, *Conquistadors in North American History*. Farrar, Straus, 1963.

*Lewis, Meriwether, *The Lewis and Clark Expedition* (3 vols.). Lippincott, 1961.

Teale, Edwin Way, *The Wilderness World of John Muir*. Houghton Mifflin, 1954.

*Wiley, Farida A., ed., *Ernest Thompson Seton's America*. Devin-Adair, 1954.

Indian History

Driver, Harold E., *Indians of North America*. University of Chicago Press, 1961.

Indiana Historical Society, *Walam Olum*. 1954.

Jennings, Jesse D., and Edward Norbeck, eds., *Prehistoric Man in the New World*. University of Chicago Press, 1964.

Kluckhohn, Clyde K., and Dorothea C. Leighton, *The Navaho* (rev. ed.). Doubleday, 1962.

**Macgowan, Kenneth, and Joseph L. Hester, Jr., *Early Man in the New World* (rev. ed.). Doubleday, 1962.

Martin, Paul S., and others, *Indians before Columbus*. University of Chicago Press, 1947.

McCracken, Harold, *George Catlin and the Old Frontier*. Dial, 1959.

Mammals

Bourlière, François, *The Natural History of Mammals* (rev. ed.). Alfred A. Knopf, 1956.

Burt, William Henry, and Richard Philip Grossenheider, *A Field Guide to the Mammals* (2nd ed.). Houghton Mifflin, 1964.

Cahalane, Victor H., *Mammals of North America*. Macmillan, 1947.

Hall, E. Raymond, and Keith R. Kelson, *The Mammals of North America* (2 vols.). Ronald Press, 1959.

Hamilton, William J., Jr., *The Mammals of Eastern United States*. Hafner, 1963.

Jackson, Hartley H. T., *Mammals of Wisconsin*. University of Wisconsin Press, 1961.

Scheffer, Victor B., *Seals, Sea Lions and Walruses*. Stanford University Press, 1958.

Storer, Tracy I., and Lloyd P. Tevis, Jr., *California Grizzly*. University of California Press, 1955.

Taylor, Walter P., ed., *The Deer of North America*. Wildlife Management Institute, 1956.

*Young, Stanley P., and Edward A. Goldman, *The Wolves of North America*. American Wildlife Institute, 1944.

Plants

**Dana, Mrs. William Starr, *How to Know the Wildflowers* (rev. ed.). Dover, 1963.

Daubenmire, R. F., *Plants and Environment* (2nd ed.). John Wiley & Sons, 1959.

†Harlow, William M., *Trees of the Eastern United States and Canada*. Dover, 1957.

**Harrar, Ellwood S., and J. George, *Guide to Southern Trees*. Dover, 1946.

Lemmon, Robert S., and Charles C. Johnson, *Wildflowers of North America*. Doubleday, 1961.

**Sargent, Charles Sprague, *Manual of the Trees of North America* (2 vols.). Dover, 1949.

Birds

Alexander, W. B., *Birds of the Ocean* (rev. ed.). G. P. Putnam's Sons, 1963.

Allen, Robert Porter, *Birds of the Caribbean*. Viking Press, 1961.

Austin, Oliver L., Jr., *Birds of the World*. Golden Press, 1961.

†Bent, Arthur Cleveland, *Life Histories of North American Birds*. Dover (continuing project on all North American species).

Check-List of North American Birds. American Ornithologists' Union, 1957.

Craighead, John J. and Frank C., *Hawks, Owls and Wildlife*. Wildlife Management Institute, 1956.

Fisher, James, and R. M. Lockley, *Sea-Birds*. Houghton Mifflin, 1954.

Ford, Alice, ed., *The Bird Biographies of John James Audubon*. Macmillan, 1957.

Gilliard, E. Thomas, *Living Birds of the World*. Doubleday, 1958.

Greenway, James C., Jr., *Extinct and Vanishing Birds of the World*. American Committee for International Wild Life Protection, 1958.

Grossman, Mary Louise, and John Hamlet, *Birds of Prey of the World*. Clarkson N. Potter, 1964.

Murphy, Robert C., and Dean Amadon, *Land Birds of America*. McGraw-Hill, 1953.

Peterson, Roger Tory, *Birds over America* (rev. ed.). Dodd, Mead, 1964.

Fish and Reptiles

Breder, Charles M., Jr., *Field Book of Marine Fishes of the Atlantic Coast* (rev. ed.). G. P. Putnam's Sons, 1948.

Ditmars, Raymond L., *The Reptiles of North America*. Doubleday, Doran, 1936.

Klauber, Laurence M., *Rattlesnakes* (2 vols.). University of California Press, 1956.

Lanham, Url, *The Fishes*. Columbia University Press, 1962.

Schmidt, Karl P., and Robert F. Inger, *Living Reptiles of the World*. Doubleday, 1957.

Schrenkeisen, Ray, *Field Book of Fresh-Water Fishes of North America*. G. P. Putnam's Sons, 1963.

Miscellaneous

Bates, Marston, *Animal Worlds*. Random House, 1963.

Hubbs, Carl L., ed., *Zoogeography*. American Association for the Advancement of Science, 1958.

Kendeigh, S. Charles, *Animal Ecology*. Prentice-Hall, 1961.

Leopold, Aldo Starker, *Wildlife of Mexico*. University of California Press, 1959.

*Matthiessen, Peter, *Wildlife in America*. Viking, 1959.

*Peterson, Roger Tory, and James Fisher, *Wild America*. Houghton Mifflin, 1955.

Shelford, Victor E., *The Ecology of North America*. University of Illinois Press, 1963.

Teale, Edwin Way, *Autumn across America*, 1956. *Journey into Summer*, 1960. *North with the Spring*, 1951. Dodd, Mead.

Udall, Stewart L., *The Quiet Crisis*. Holt, Rinehart and Winston, 1963.

---

* Also available in paperback.
† Only available in paperback.
** Also available in hard cover.

Index

Numerals in italics indicate a photograph or painting of the subject mentioned.

Index, *continued*

PRODUCTION STAFF FOR TIME INCORPORATED

Arthur R. Murphy Jr. (Vice President and Director of Production), Robert E. Foy, James P. Menton, Caroline Ferri and Robert E. Fraser
Text photocomposed under the direction of Albert J. Dunn and Arthur J. Dunn

x

Printed by R. R. Donnelley & Sons Company, Crawfordsville, Indiana,
and by Livermore and Knight Co., a division of Printing Corporation of America, Providence, Rhode Island
Bound by R. R. Donnelley & Sons Company, Crawfordsville, Indiana
Paper by The Mead Corporation, Dayton, Ohio
Cover stock by The Plastic Coating Corporation, Holyoke, Massachusetts